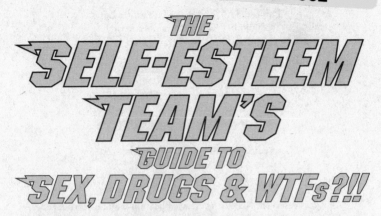

THE SELF-ESTEEM TEAM'S GUIDE TO SEX, DRUGS & WTFs?!!

WITH A FOREWORD BY ZOELLA

GRACE BARRETT • NATASHA DEVON • NADIA MENDOZA

JOHN BLAKE

Published by John Blake Publishing Ltd,
3 Bramber Court, 2 Bramber Road,
London W14 9PB, England

www.johnblakebooks.com

www.facebook.com/johnblakebooks

twitter.com/jblakebooks

This edition published in paperback in 2015

ISBN: 978 1 78418 642 5

British Library Cataloguing-in-Publication Data:

A catalogue record for this book is available from the British Library.

Design by www.envydesign.co.uk

Printed in Great Britain by CPI Group (UK) Ltd

1 3 5 7 9 10 8 6 4 2

Papers used by John Blake Publishing are natural, recyclable products made
from wood grown in sustainable forests. The manufacturing processes
conform to the environmental regulations of the country of origin.

Every attempt has been made to contact the relevant copyright-holders,
but some were unobtainable. We would be grateful if the
appropriate people could contact us.

Dedicated to the 50,000 teenagers we've worked
with since 2008, who are the actual experts.
Your feedback keeps our classes fresh.
Knowing you gives us hope for the future.

Love,
The Self-Esteem Team

THE
SELF-ESTEEM
TEAM'S
GUIDE TO
SEX, DRUGS & WTFs?!!

CONTENTS

FOREWORD BY ZOELLA

I have been lucky to have fallen into a career that inspires others all over the world. Of course, I am eternally thankful, but anyone who watches my YouTube channel will know I also struggle with anxiety. It doesn't matter how successful you are, or how happy you might appear on the outside, everyone battles secret demons from time-to-time. It's just part of being a human being.

Since talking about my own struggles, thousands of teenagers have contacted me to tell me that they too are fighting feelings they find hard to understand. Whether it's because they have been bullied, have lost someone they love, have problems at home, or they simply don't know why, when I described how anxiety felt to me, a lot of people could relate.

It's for that reason I'm so thrilled The Self-Esteem Team (and this book) exist. The Self-Esteem Team give the message that it's OK to be you, that individuality is cool, and that you don't have to face your troubles alone. They are tackling the mental-health crisis head-on in a way that is accessible, down-to-earth, and even fun. Most importantly, they base what they say not only on personal experience, but having spoken to (and continuing conversation with) tens of thousands of real teens. They are a megaphone for the voice of young people and are answering real concerns on what they hear.

Without the Internet, I wouldn't be the person I am today. Yet it also presents unique challenges. It's hard to remember that you are a great and beautiful human in a never-ending world of Photoshopped selfies and trolls who have direct access to your phone. Sometimes, we all need to be reminded that nobody is perfect and that we are loved and valued just as we are.

I hope this book will help you to remember those things. It's a survival guide for the modern age, packed with pearls of wisdom, real anecdotes and witty musings. At times it will make you laugh out loud, but it might also make you cry. Either way, carry it with you; there's a strategy or word of advice for almost every dilemma faced by today's teens. And even I, at twenty-five, can continue learning from it.

Enjoy, and be proud to be you.
Love Zoella

ABOUT THIS BOOK

There are certain questions in life you wouldn't necessarily ask your parents, can't really ask your teachers and definitely shouldn't Google. Things like 'What's the difference between porn and real sex?' 'What's it like to take drugs?' and 'Seriously, what's the worst that could happen…?'

You could try asking your friends but they probably don't know either and might just make something up to try and look clever (which is how urban myths about people getting stuck together during sex started. It. Never. Happened. Trust). Ideally, what you need for these kinds of discussions is a knowledgeable Big Sister type character but a) not everyone has a big sister and b) older siblings tend to be really busy rebelling/

defiantly pushing the boundaries of what your parents consider to be acceptable behaviour.

So that's why this book happened. The Self-Esteem Team (the Universal Big Sisters to young people across the globe) answer the questions that the thousands of teenagers they have met during the course of their work have asked most often.

The Self-Esteem Team each have jobs in showbiz/ media and so understand exactly how bizarre the modern world can be. They have met a lot of important experts, attended A LOT of (often fist-gnawingly dull) conferences and, between them, they know quite a bit about mental health and body image. But more importantly, they also remember what it was like to be a teenager and how being patronised made them want to kick the wall while making an 'UHHHHHH!!!' noise.

So what you will find is that their answers are honest, sometimes funny, full of compassion and occasionally a bit sweary – because there is no reason why they shouldn't talk to you in the same way they talk to each other (which is always honest, funny, compassionate and a bit sweary).

The Self-Esteem Team hope this book helps you be the best version of you, while rocking your own unique brand of gorgeous, so you can successfully navigate this crazy thing we call life...

INTRODUCING THE SELF-ESTEEM TEAM

TASH

My name is Natasha Devon (Tash to my friends – which includes you, reader) and I'm a writer, columnist for *Cosmopolitan* magazine and TV pundit (the TV thing sounds glamorous but actually it just means I spend a lot of time sitting on sofas arguing about politics with middle-aged men wearing Marks & Spencer suits).

Being opinionated has always been the defining element of my personality. I am sometimes described as 'scary' but really I'm just passionate about pretty much everything (I've been known to 'passionately not give a shit' on occasion), have a massively overdeveloped sense of fairness and like to talk.

At school, a combination of having *all* the opinions in the world, being a huge swot and needing to be the best at *everything* didn't make me particularly popular (I know: shocking). If I'm totally honest, I didn't particularly mind not having many friends. Mates weren't really the point of school for me. I used to watch some of the other people in my year – who clearly used school mainly as a social opportunity, spending their time gossiping on low walls between classrooms and giggling over a cigarette behind the gym block – and think, 'WOT?'

I loved learning for learning's sake. I was never that person in class who said 'But Miss, how is this relevant to life?' It wouldn't have even occurred to me to ask that question. Everything interested me. I always had my nose in a book, even when I was walking around, which often meant I bumped into things, like a total tit. I was the one who used to request extra homework. I'm sure you have someone who does this in your year (and you probably hate them, which is totally understandable. If I wasn't me, I would have hated me).

I am testament to the fact that, if you just carry on being yourself, eventually you will become cool. The people that used to tease me at school for being 'weird' have since got in touch on Facebook, telling me they've read something I've written or seen me on TV and want to congratulate me on inspiring them with my opinions. What was, for so long, the thing that marked me out as being 'different' is now what I do for a living.

There was, however, a significant period of time when I wasn't myself and those were the worst years of my life. Shortly after starting university, I simultaneously discovered sexual attention and 50p shots of vodka. I lost my way, making a hugely ill-advised leap into modelling, abandoning my love of writing, books and being opinionated to instead sit in nightclubs, looking pretty on the arm of a bloke who couldn't even remember my name, let alone bring himself to respect me. Like a lot of people, I bought into the idea that, if I could only be 'beautiful' (which I had interpreted as being as thin as possible), life would be easier and I would be better, happier and more successful.

I became someone I didn't recognise or like. I was superficial, vacuous, attention-seeking – drama followed me wherever I went. I punished myself for not having the willpower to starve myself or to fit in with the 'in crowd' but, more than that, I hated myself for even wanting those things in the first place. I made myself sick, drank until I blacked out, exercised until I felt faint – anything that would make me forget, at least temporarily, that I was squandering my potential in the pursuit of something that didn't exist.

Eight years after leaving school, I had no job, no money, no friends and nothing to show for my life. This is despite having been a straight-A student, which just goes to show that exams aren't everything.

I realised that school shouldn't just be about academia or getting qualifications – an education should prepare you for life. After recovering from the eating disorder I'd sacrificed almost a decade to, I created The Self-Esteem Team, a group consisting of myself and two of my favourite people in the world: Grace Barrett and Nadia Mendoza (aka Nadz). We visit schools and teach young people about the things that are *really* vital to your success and happiness – things like maintaining good mental health, having a positive relationship with your body and knowing and liking who you are.

I realise, of course, that you are probably reading this thinking, 'Well, if she had an eating disorder and ended up writing for *Cosmo*, they can't be that bad.' I want you to beat that thought to death. Extinguish it forever from your mind. I was very lucky that I was able, with the support of my friends and family, to pull myself back from the edge of the precipice. Millions of people waste their lives, spend all their days in painful misery, get caught in a cycle of endless hospitalisations or even die because of eating disorders.

But more than that, I missed out on so much – years of my life I can never claim back. I know being a teenager can be really frustrating a lot of the time (because, in many cases, you actually *do* know better than the adult you're arguing with but they get to win anyway) but there's also more than a nugget of truth in the idea that these are the best years of your life. You are finding out who you are and that's an incredibly exciting and important journey.

You are destined during these years to make friends with the most interesting people you will ever meet, have conversations that will blow your mind, fall in love and have your heart broken for the first time (it won't actually kill you, even though it will definitely feel like it), maybe travel, study something that properly interests you or earn your first pay cheque (it's an amazing feeling). That's what your teens and early twenties are for. I spent mine with my head in a toilet.

It's that thought that gets me out of bed to travel to far-flung corners of the UK at 4am on a cold winter's morning to deliver a class while attempting to meet my column deadline by furiously bashing at my laptop on the train journey. If that class helps at least one person, that's one person who might not make the kinds of mistakes I did and will be empowered to achieve the most amazing feat of all: being happy.

GRACE

Hello! I'm Grace and I grew up as an eczema-ridden, mixed-race freak (freaky because in the 1990s in Stoke-on-Trent there were next to no people 'of colour' – in my school, my brother and I made up the lion's share). My mum had to make the decision to shave my head because I'd pulled great lumps of hair out while scratching my scalp in the night (yum) and I was wrapped in bandages a lot of the time due to the skin condition. I also had a speech impediment (that made me pronounce my name 'Gwayth') and feet that turned inwards. Oddly enough, these differences never really made me a target for bullies but I did feel *agonisingly* alone and hyper aware of every confused look thrown in my direction, which added to my feelings of isolation.

I always knew that I would be a performer and, in my head, that meant becoming someone who had perfect skin, long flowing locks and loads of people around just like me, which would help me fit in. I didn't think about how I'd get there or the stuff in between, I just assumed that it would happen.

So when I left the Midlands to start my career as a London-based singer and entered one of the most judgemental industries on earth, still covered in eczema, with incredibly un-flowing locks and not a single girl in the audition room who looked like me, I was forced to find a bit of self-esteem. I very quickly learned the balance between confidence and arrogance and the importance of knowing your weaknesses, asking for help and that sometimes you really do have to fake it until you feel it. I'm happy to say that I think I nearly have that balance right.

While travelling around the world with bands (musicians by the way, despite their brilliance, ego, talent and bravado, collectively have the lowest self-esteem of any group of people I've ever met), I've picked up some tips, as well as the unshakeable knowledge that beauty is bullshit. Every country has a different definition of what beauty means, which essentially makes it a moo point ('it's like a cow's opinion: it doesn't matter' – Joey Tribbiani, ladies and gents) and confidence is rare yet golden – because those that really have it light up the room – and my life along with it.

So now, as one third of The Self-Esteem Team, I'm touring again. This time, around schools to share some of the wisdom and tips that I've learned and to show people that it really is OK to be yourself in a world that often demands you to conform.

NADZ

Every time I stand in front of a class to deliver The Self-Esteem Team workshop, I shit bricks. My heart races, I need the loo 3,085,435 times beforehand, my hands go clammy, my mouth goes dry and the words don't come out unless I rely heavily on my notes. But afterwards, when teens come

up to me to say I have opened their eyes, made them feel better or have inspired them to seek help, it is worth every nanosecond of enduring that anxiety.

Not talking about my problems is what plunged me into the blackest of depressions and left me battling a self-harm addiction, as I felt I had no one to turn to. I was afraid telling someone would go one of two ways: being dismissed and told to 'pull myself together' or being locked up in a psychiatric unit. There was also the small fact that I didn't actually want to get better. Other classmates were good at guitar, or football, or getting straight As; I was 'good' at being ill. No matter how hard it is, I now know being open on mental health is the first step to getting well again.

It is still uncomfortable to speak about what happened to me and the words sound ugly and fucked-up coming out. I can't tell you what went through my head as I picked up the scissors that very first time on a random day in Year 7 but I can tell you that it shut out all the chaos for just one moment. It silenced the bullies. It made the difficulties at home magic into nowhere. It allowed me to cry without tears. While I didn't understand it at the time (I still struggle to), it seemed to externalise what was going on inside. Yet what I romanticised as the 'friend' that helped me was also the devil that stole me. It took away my voice, leaving me stuck on a merry-go-round of bottling things in and bleeding them out. And so, for a very,

very long time, I spoke through my skin because I couldn't find the right words.

Things began turning around for me when I went to uni. I accepted that I needed therapy and began taking anti-depressants properly, not just for a month here or there then being too drunk to turn up at the doctor for my next prescription. I started to use writing as a way to let the feelings out and also learned to use my body in a positive, rather than negative, way to express myself; experimenting with clothes, tattoos, even my hair, to tell my story. While bright-pink dye may look like a symbol of confidence, for me it represents loneliness. It's my way of saying I don't fit in – a version of raising the barriers before people get to me.

When I landed a job as a showbiz journalist for Britain's best-selling tabloid, it was beyond a dream. Not just because my career took me to the bright lights of Hollywood, or interviewing celebs, or raving at music festivals, but because it was the ultimate tool of self-belief, as I had found a thrill in writing and started carving out my own niche in life.

Yet it's being part of The Self-Esteem Team that is greater than walking any red carpet or drinking a free bottle of champagne at an awards ceremony; the chance to share my experiences and reach out to teenagers who are struggling with feelings they find difficult to communicate and deal with.

No matter how stubborn I am in sentimentalising

self-harm as something that 'helped' me – and no matter how reluctant I am in having had to give it up – it was only recovery that saved me from myself. It can still be a steep hill to climb but I try to wear my scars with pride. They are a part of me, something I picked up along life's journey, part of my story. But I know I cherished self-harm more than it ever did me. Now, I hope to speak for all the young people out there who feel like they aren't 'cool' enough, to show you positive and creative ways to stick two fingers up at your demons, whatever they may be.

Here goes...

CHAPTER ONE

IF I HAVE HIGH SELF-ESTEEM, WILL I BECOME ARROGANT?

GRACE

I've been thinking about this question of arrogance for a few weeks (well, longer because we're asked it a lot). I've been thinking about it while I'm on the bus or in supermarkets or in dance class (I nearly fell over in class actually because I wasn't concentrating on my feet enough... in fact, I fall over quite a lot *blush*) and every time I think about it, the answer that comes into my head is: 'No, you won't, it doesn't work like that. Just... no.'

But I realise that's not really enough of an answer, so try this...

High self-esteem is really easy to spot when you know what it looks like but it's also really easy to confuse for other stuff when you don't – a bit like love. True love

1

is kind, caring, freeing and not jealous. Infatuation can look a lot like love but it's completely different. It is caring, to a point, but it's restricting instead of freeing and it is jealous beyond belief. This analogy is almost exactly the same as self-esteem vs. arrogance.

People who possess self-esteem are able to be kind and caring to others because they know that doing that won't mean they have any less kindness and care for themselves. They feel free to be themselves but not to impose that on other people and, most of all, they are not jealous, because they have no need to be – difference is exciting to them and unintimidating. Yes, that person may be hotter than me and have qualities I don't possess but that works both ways. I'll have qualities that they don't and that's enough for me to know I have value.

When you feel that way, there's no need to put anybody else down or prove your worth in a room.

It's also important to remember that high self-esteem rarely happens by accident. It's a safe bet that someone with loads of it has had to go on a bit of a journey in order to acquire it (and they'll constantly be doing things to maintain it too), so they can normally empathise and see things from someone else's point of view.

I could ramble on like this endlessly because there are so many reasons why arrogance and self-esteem are completely different. But for now, I'll just say 'No, you won't because it just doesn't work like that,' and hand over to Nadz...

NADZ

If Self-Esteem and Arrogance were people, they'd probably hang out in the same circles and know the same folk but they wouldn't be close. Arrogance would be pals with Cocky, Ego and Smug, while Self-Esteem would be mates with Hope, Positivity and Fuck-Yeah. While both parties seem to be on a yellow-brick road to confidence, there is a glaring difference: Self-esteem smiles, Arrogance smirks.

Having self-esteem then catapulting into arrogance territory is about as likely as Kim Kardashian surrendering selfies forever. Ain't gonna happen. Self-esteem means having self-awareness, liking yourself but also having respect for others. It means knowing you still have things to learn, listening to other people, being open-minded and optimistic, as well as realistic.

Arrogance, however, lacks self-awareness. It means a disrespect for others, not listening and not learning from people, nor being open-minded. It means being unrealistic, conceited in opinion and pessimistic in outlook, with the arrogant person believing they are always right. In a nutshell, the two are polar opposites.

Just as a self-aware person is unlikely to be struck by arrogance, the arrogant person is unlikely to have self-esteem. In fact, they probably have a deep fear of exposing their vulnerability (something the person with self-esteem would not mind, as they understand it doesn't make them look weak). It teeters on bully mentality; putting others down to big themselves up. Think of a cyberbully: the arrogance they have to lash out online may make them seem confident but it's highly unlikely they have much self-esteem if they have to slate others.

Also, self-esteem doesn't mean being so confident that you never worry again. I have self-esteem in that I wear what I want, don't really follow a crowd and don't post a lot on social media to get reassurance from likes, but I am also insecure over what people say behind my back, if I look ugly on a 'bad face day' and if I sound stupid when I speak, as I'm not particularly good at articulating myself.

Note from Tash: Nadz is *incredibly* good at articulating herself and has been asked to see me after school for Self-Esteem Detention.

Self-esteem is accepting what you cannot change, having the courage to change the things you can and having the wisdom to know the difference.

Arrogance is thinking nothing needs changing.

TASH

I get asked the arrogance question a lot, usually by slightly sneery TV journalists who think it's funny to say, 'Some people would argue that young people today have too much confidence and no respect for their elders – they don't need a self-esteem class, they need a big dose of humility. Bring back the cane, I say!' *mwahhahahaha SNARF SNARF SNARF*.

Let us be clear: self-esteem means having the confidence to be yourself, whether you are naturally outgoing or more reserved. The person with the most confidence in a room isn't necessarily the loudest or the person who is quickest to challenge authority. Sometimes, the person with the highest self-esteem is the one who can just sit and listen to what everyone else is saying and take a moment to enjoy being alive.

When I was at my lowest, self-esteem wise, I was an absolute bitch. I used to walk around with my nose in the air, pouting, judging everyone else and secretly wondering why no one liked me. I used to seek attention in the worst possible ways because I didn't care why everyone was looking in my direction, just so long as I was the focus.

From the outside, I have no doubt that people thought of me as 'arrogant', yet all I wanted was to feel like it was OK to be me and that I could relax. I remember saying to my dad, 'I just want to be someone,' and him looking confused and replying, 'But you *are* someone, love.' And that was the issue: I couldn't see that I was even a person – I felt like an angry mess of pent-up emotions and incidents of fuckuppery, surviving from moment to moment.

Self-esteem doesn't just give you the confidence to strive for the things you really want, it's also what allows you to be content with what you have. Self-esteem is the thing that makes you understand what drives and motivates you, to be genuinely happy for other people's triumphs and to forgive yourself, learn and move on from your failures. (It is also sexy. FACT.)

Gaining self-esteem was, for me, realising that I am truly unique, brilliant and special... and so is everyone else.

In essence, you can never have too much self-esteem and anyone who tells you differently doesn't actually understand what it is. So there.

CHAPTER TWO

'I DON'T FEEL 'RIGHT'

NADZ

At the first school I ever taught in with The Self-Esteem Team, a Year 9 student came up to me after my lesson to say, 'I don't feel right,' before bursting into tears. I just hugged her and tried to tell her that everything was going to be OK. While I can never know exactly how it feels to be in her shoes, I understand what it's like to feel as though your skin doesn't fit and that you are grotesquely abnormal from the rest of society.

But what the hell is normal anyway? And if we can't answer that, how do we know what abnormal is? Let's say that not feeling right is when you feel different from how you've been feeling in life up until that point. So that would mean that feeling abnormal doesn't mean the same thing to everyone. In fact, feeling abnormal

7

is really normal because it happens to every human at some stage. You'd need to feel abnormal from time to time in order to be normal, which means we're all really normal... this explanation sounds normal in my head but not so normal written down... The more I type 'normal', the more it sounds less normal. ARGH! Is it normal to write 'normal' so much in one normal paragraph?!! #normal

Epic brain fart.

Seriously though, you can only feel what you feel. Emotions aren't by choice; in fact, they are the very opposite. Feelings stick to you with zero choice at all, whizzing around your brain at a million miles per hour. What *is* your choice is how you then deal with them, whether you allow them to consume you or whether you choose to conquer them. So when you feel like something is not right, that's OK. It's the steps you take after that count.

It feels horrible when someone asks 'What's wrong?' when all you can think is 'What's right?' Yet what you can do is learn how to manage your feelings by sowing seeds of confidence, instead of weeds of doubt, in your brain.

First, know that difficult emotions are a flaw in chemistry, not in character, so try not to beat yourself up. Second, you are not weird. Promise. Depression, self-doubt and insecurities all stem from feelings, which we all have (even people who seem secure). Third, it's about programming the mind to realise you *can*, rather than believing you can't.

TASH

When people say they don't 'feel right', what they usually mean is, 'Something's wrong, but I don't know what it is.'

You'd be surprised by how many people experience a kind of general 'blah' type feeling but can't attribute it to anything specific. One of two things then happens:

1. They either try to make how they are feeling fit something – anything that's happened recently ('My friend's budgie has early-onset diabetes and I'm just *so* cut up about it!').
2. They convince themselves they don't have the 'right' to 'feel sorry for themselves' and try to swallow down their emotions and soldier on.

Both of these tactics are diversionary – they stop you from getting to the root of the problem and mean that whatever it is that's really bothering you will fester and grow.

If you feel insecure, or are behaving in ways you don't recognise or like (like flying off the handle or sulking if you don't get your own way), it means you have sunk into bad habits. Habits are powerful because they are so subtle; they creep up on us. We repeat negative patterns of thought or behaviour without really being aware that we're doing it, then, before we know it, we 'don't feel right' but we have no idea why.

There's a couple of ways you can combat this. The first is to try to identify how the habit started. This is useful because, if you can cast your mind back to what was happening during the time you started to think or behave in negative ways, it'll give you a massive hint as to what's bugging you.

Human beings have 'defence mechanisms' built into us, which make it easier for us to cope with difficult situations while they are actually happening. So you can be going through something that should technically be difficult to deal with – like a bereavement or a break-up – and think 'Hey! I'm dealing with this *so well*. Check me out being all mature and shit!' but actually, your defence mechanisms have kicked in, meaning you're having a sort of out-of-body experience. When this happens, we put all the toxic emotions we don't want to deal with into a box at the back of our minds, to be reopened at a later date, when everything has settled down. So it can be weeks, months or even years later when those emotions re-emerge and it's so unexpected that you're left thinking, 'What The Actual F?'

Equally, however, it could be nothing like as dramatic as that. And that's also fine. You can't help how you feel. So if your friend's budgie having diabetes really and genuinely has affected you, it's OK to feel sad. Go ahead and wail into a pillow.

This shouldn't be confused with giving yourself permission to wallow in self-pity though. I had a friend who did that once and she made it really hard for her mates to be around her. She was seeing this bloke she really liked for about three months when he dumped her with no real explanation. *Two years later* she was still talking about it. *Every* time I saw her. And when I gently suggested that perhaps it was time to move on, she'd say, 'Tash, I can't help how I feeeeeel!'

Obviously, you want to avoid behaving in this dramatic manner if you can. The way to do that is to identify the emotion, give yourself some time to deal with it and then work out how you're going to move forward.

Like Nadz said, you can't control how you feel but you *can* control how you deal with it.

Over to Grace, who is going to talk tactics for pulling yourself out of the slump...

GRACE

Sometimes, looking back can be really useful. Working out the root cause of a problem is important. But if you're in a negative place ('OMG, I can't connect to wifi – can the world *just give me a break*!?'), it's possible that looking back will only result in a ride on the Brain-Worm of Doom. Yeah, that's the pet name I give my neggy thoughts.

So instead, work forwards. Try focusing not on what the problem is but what the solution could be. Work out what feeling 'right' might be to you. I'm not saying you'll be able to work that out in a matter of minutes, hours or even days but I do think it's a more useful way of spending time than thinking 'What's wrong (with me, the world, my friends, my family...)?' The list could be endless.

Imagine yourself feeling 'right' – or even let's go so far as to say feeling happy *gasp*! Or remember the last time you felt that way. Got it? Good. Now picture it. Look at the scene: what's around you? What are you doing? What does it sound like? Who are you with? Most importantly, what are the differences between the way your world actually looks and feels to the one you're imagining? Scribble them down if you need to. Now, what can you do to make your world look and feel more like the one you're imagining?

Sometimes, the most useful question to ask is: 'What would I like to happen?'

It took me quite a while to answer that question for myself, back when I didn't feel 'right'. But once I realised that my ideal scene was really quite different to the one I was living, the feeling made complete sense. I still don't get to spend every single day in my 'perfect world' but, in trying to make mine look more like the one I'd imagined, I normally tick a couple of its boxes each day.

These days, it's much rarer that I don't feel right. I still have wobbles (I think everyone does) but much less often – and when I do have one, I can now envisage a way to clamber out of that hole.

CHAPTER THREE

HOW DO I KNOW IF I'M HEALTHY?

(INCLUDING 'WHAT'S A NORMAL WEIGHT/SIZE FOR SOMEONE MY AGE?' AND 'HOW MUCH SHOULD I BE EATING AND EXERCISING?')

TASH

No matter what I do, my body just refuses to dip below a certain size (I could, of course, die trying to reach that elusive goal but, fortunately, these days I have more important shit to be getting on with).

When I was a model, my naturally large frame was seen as a bit of an issue for my employers. Particularly as, at the time, the fashion industry operated a 'No such thing as too thin' policy (it was the late 1990s and there was something called 'heroin chic', which is a contradiction in terms if ever I heard one).

I was quite often wheeled out as an example of a 'healthy' model because I was a couple of sizes larger than the people you tend to see on catwalks. This was utterly twatting preposterous because, lest we forget, at that time in my life, I was in the grips of a severe eating disorder. I was about as unhealthy as a person can get, both physically and mentally. And some (although not many) of the models who were thinner than me and were called 'unhealthy' were just naturally built that way and ate very well indeed.

The point of me telling you this is to demonstrate that it's largely impossible to gauge whether someone is healthy or not just by looking at them. Health is defined by lifestyle, not looks.

The problem is that there are lots of people who go about their quest to 'be healthy' in totally the wrong way because they think health is achieved at a certain size, or defined by being super-muscly. This happens for two reasons:

1. Medical professionals have to have some parameters for defining whether someone is healthy, so they created what's called a BMI (Body Mass Index) chart. This divides into five sections: Underweight, Normal, Overweight, Obese and Morbidly Obese. If you are either side of 'normal' your doctor may very well advise you to either lose or gain weight. With NHS GPs under increasing pressure to see a gazillion patients every day, they'll often weigh people and make a snap judgement on their health, rather than doing

more in-depth investigations (like blood tests).

2. A few years ago, the beauty, fitness and fashion industries got wind of the fact that everyone was really fed up of being told they must be thin all the time and started banging on endlessly about 'health'. Celeb magazines started using phrases like 'Such-and-such is now a healthy size 10!!' to try and mask their awful body-shaming tactics as something more worthy. It's also a really convenient and powerful way to make people buy certain products, whether it's a calorie-free drink, protein powder or even cosmetic surgery. 'Buy this and you'll be healthy!' sits better with the consumer than 'Buy this and you'll be really attractive and everyone will love you!' (Both are lies but one is less obviously a lie.)

BMI

I wrote an article once called 'The B in BMI stands for Bullshit', which should tell you everything you need to know about my stance on it. It's *kind of* useful as a very broad guide (in that it's not fantastic for your health if you're either extremely underweight or morbidly obese) but there are so many exceptions to who falls outside the 'normal' section. To give just a few examples:

- Black and mixed-race people tend to have more muscle density, so are often classed as 'overweight' when the briefest glance in their direction would show that they're not. (A black friend of mine went through school being teased by his classmates for being 'skinny', while being told by his doctor he was 'overweight' – which would be laughable if it wasn't so tragic.)
- Professional athletes – particularly rugby players or people who do sports that cause you to 'bulk up' – can be 'obese', according to a BMI chart, despite being (obviously) really fit and healthy.
- Bone structure can have an impact at both ends of the scale. There *is* such a thing as 'big boned' – having broad shoulders, wide hips, big feet, etc. indicates that your bones literally weigh a lot. Equally, having a small frame is likely to put you in the 'underweight' section, even if you eat really well.

Bodies vary enormously. If you want the scientific explanation, it's all to do with evolution because different body types had different skills that, collectively, ensured our survival (which is why some people are really good at running – their ancestors were catching bison – and some people are very strong – their ancestors were bludgeoning the bison to death). So lots of variants of 'Homo sapiens' (posh word for human beings) survived and created different 'lineages' (posh word for children who look like them) that still exist today. Some people are naturally slender, with really fast metabolisms (so burn off any food they consume almost instantly), while others are destined to be a little heavier.

Trying to create a BMI chart that caters for all these different body types is, as I said in the beginning, BULL. SHIT.

MINDFUL EATING

The key to healthy eating is to tune into your body and learn to listen to it.

When you were a baby, you knew exactly when you were hungry and you stopped drinking milk when you were full. Hunger is an instinct. Yet over time, we start to eat for different reasons: because we are bored, happy, lonely, celebrating or anxious. Or we deny ourselves food because our emotional brains have decided that's the best thing. What this does is mess with your body's internal balance. Your body is a magnificent, self-regulating machine – if you trust it, it will remain at a weight that is healthy for you. It's all about distinguishing between genuine hunger (when your body needs fuel) and what's called 'emotional hunger' (when your mind tells you to eat for another reason).

I should say at this point that it's best not to eat loads of really highly processed foods, or foods with a high sugar content (which, I am sorry to have to tell you, includes swerving the chicken shop). That's because these foods are highly addictive and you crave them in the same way you might crave a drug, but they aren't giving you much in the way of nutritional value. It's OK to have them once in a while, as a treat, but having them every day is bad for anyone, regardless of whether it causes you to gain weight.

Aside from foods which are addictive, cravings are there for a reason. For example, a lot of women crave chocolate either during or directly prior to their period. That's because chocolate has iron in it (especially dark chocolate) and your body knows it's about to lose blood and is trying to stop you from becoming anaemic. Clever, hey?

I like to practice something called 'mindful eating', which is designed to stop you overeating just for the sake of it (like when you're watching a film and suddenly you think 'WHO ATE ALL MY MALTESERS?') Mindful eating is when you take time to really notice and enjoy your food. So, for example, I always arrange my meals nicely on a plate, I sit down to eat and try to avoid distractions (phones, laptops, TV, etc.). I eat slowly and put my knife and fork down between each bite. Obviously, there are days when I'm super busy and mindful eating is impossible because I'm running around trying to save the world, but it's a good habit to get into when you can. It definitely helped me to recover from my eating disorder because it allowed me to resist the urge to binge eat by being in control of what I was doing.

If you want to find out more about mindful eating, check out an amazing organisation called Beyond Chocolate – details at the back of this book.

EXERCISE

You can apply the 'mindful eating' theory to exercise – people who are really in tune with their bodies know when they need to expend some energy (by dancing around their living room to Beyoncé in their pants/ another form of physical exertion) and when they need to conserve it (by sitting on their arse). As a very general rule, experts reckon teenagers should do about half an hour of exercise per day (although that can vary if you are training for something specific).

In just the same way as health isn't defined by size, strength isn't necessarily denoted by muscles. There are two types of muscles – ones you can see from the outside (which are largely for show) and ones you can't, which are actually the ones that make you genuinely strong. Pasha Kovalev, one of the professional dancers on *Strictly Come Dancing*, is a good friend of mine and, if you Google him, you'll see he appears quite slender. He can lift a fully grown woman with one arm.

It's worth noting here too that, just as there are muscles you can't see, there is also something called 'visceral fat'. This is fat that sits around your organs but is invisible to the naked eye. So it's possible to look slim but have visceral fat, which is the type that actually makes you more susceptible to heart disease, etc. The best way to avoid visceral fat is not to eat too much processed, saturated fat (found in fast foods). However, natural fats (such as those found in olive oil, avocados and nuts) are essential for the body and, in fact, reduce your risk of heart disease – this is called 'good cholesterol'.

It's all really confusing but, basically, a good rule of thumb is 'the more natural, the better.' If you grew it in your garden, it's probably the best thing you can eat (unless it's a mushroom – which might poison you – or your mum's chrysanthemums).

PROTEIN POWDERS/ENERGY DRINKS

Protein powders were invented for professional athletes who train for several hours every day and those people continue to be the only people who really need them. Of course, the companies who make protein shakes and powders will try to persuade you that they will increase your strength/stamina/help you gain muscle/lose weight, when, in actual fact, they can't do anything for the average person that just having some scrambled eggs or some chicken couldn't. What they *can* do is cause liver and kidney failure (if you have ever peed bright yellow/green, that is your liver saying, 'HELP!

Above left: Nadz as a painfully shy teenager.

Above right: ...little did she know, one day she'd be reporting from the Oscars.

Below: Grace was good at hiding her insecurities growing up.

NATASHA DEVON
Self-esteem campaigner
BBC BREAKFAST

Above: ...but on stage there is nowhere to hide.

Below left: This is Tash's thirteenth birthday party (there were other people there, honest).

Below right: ...now, Tash has opinions for a living.

Above left: Grace and Nadz on their very first day of training, which Boss Lady Tash decided to do in the park (nice). Ice lollies out of shot.

Above right: Grace and students at The Manor School, Cambridge celebrating after performing to HRH Duke & Duchess of Cambridge (aka Will & Kate).

Below: SET on set! Filming *Teens Online* with ITV.

Above: After seeing *Teens Online* Emily Waterhouse (*centre*) invited Nadz into her school in Durham.

Below: Tash presenting an assembly at Thomas Cowley School in Lincolnshire. Nadz thinks she looks quite godlike, here. Tash thinks you can see her pants (damn you, projector lights!).

Left: Winning a Body Confidence Award at the House of Commons in November 2014, presented by comedian Juliette Burton and Radio 1 DJ Jameela Jamil.

Right: Celebrating our win with honorary SET Member/Total Legend Gok Wan.

Left: Proving that it's good to be different – Post Halloween themed photoshoot in Abney Park Cemetery with makeup by the brilliant Face-painting Fairy (and Nadz' big sister) Livi Lollipop.

Left: Our first ever magazine spread in *Fabulous* magazine… And possibly the only time we've ever been photographed not on our official 'sides'.

Below left: We leave post it notes like this in random places. Now you know, you might find one on a lamp post/train/cashpoint near you.

Below right: Supporting the Pink Ribbon Foundation for breast cancer care at their fundraiser at Gilgamesh in Camden.

The ♥ INDEPENDENT

**100 DAYS
100 PEOPLE**

**IF I WERE
PRIME
MINISTER...**

If I were Prime Minister: I'd make schools about learning skills, not facts

Our series in the run-up to the General Election – 100 days, 100 contributors, but no politicians – continues with the Founder of the Self Esteem Team

Above: #Normal.

Below left: Attending the Cosmopolitan Ultimate Women of the Year Awards in 2014 – dressed as Quality Street!

Below right: Vote Tash! Getting political and talking about how to make the education system work for all young people.

Left: Our latest campaign is called 'Switch on the Light' and is aimed at men – you can see the video starring Stephen Fry, Professor Green, TV presenter Ortis Deley, comedian Ian Royce, footballer Clarke Carlisle, Deaf Havana frontman James Veck-Gilodi and YouTube star Charlie McDonnell on SET's YouTube channel.

Right: If Grace had her way, we would have been called the 'Self E-Steam Train' (if that made you laugh, you and Grace will get on).

Left: Our motto: See no Evil, Hear no Evil, Speak no Evil.

TOO MUCH PROTEIN') and cause you to build too much 'superficial' muscle for your frame, particularly if you're still growing.

Energy drinks are even more bollocks than protein shakes. They're just processed sugar (which is bad for you) and water (which is freely available from every tap in the land). Ignore pompous claims about 'electrolytes': these have about as much meaning as conditioners that claim to 'infuse your hair shaft with nutrients' (also impossible). It's all pseudo-scientific, made-up guff.

Energy drinks can also rot your teeth, so if you do insist on drinking them, it's best to use a straw.

But really and honestly, if you're working hard and sweating a lot, having a drink of water is the best thing you can do (boring but true).

ORTHOREXIA

I won't patronise you by describing all the various food groups, telling you to get enough sleep, not smoke, etc. because you've probably known about that since you were five. What I will say is that it is all about balance. Being able to treat yourself to foods that are delicious but won't give you any nutrients once in a while is all part of a healthy mindset. Nutritionists reckon if you eat healthily 80 per cent of the time, it's OK to let yourself off the other 20 per cent – the body can cope with that. Similarly, if you're genuinely too knackered to play sport, don't. You need to rest sometimes.

When the desire to be 'healthy' becomes compulsive – i.e. you freak out if you so much as sniff a chip, or go to the gym even if you are poorly – that is actually classified as an eating disorder (in the media, it is often referred to as 'orthorexia').

BODY CONFIDENCE

If the questions I get asked during my body-image workshops are any indication, lots of people seem to think that, if they have 'body confidence', that means they'll be unhealthy, as they'll think it's fine to sit on their sofa all day eating lard, happy no matter how they look.

This is really twisted logic because, actually, people who love their bodies want to look after them. Having pride in your body is much like owning a brand-new car – because you love it, you'll want to keep it spangly and polished and fill it with the best fuel. The government did a survey in 2014 and found that 18 million people in Britain alone are too ashamed of how their bodies look to do any form of exercise. Similarly, over- or under-eating, or binge drinking, can often be a sign that we don't like ourselves very much. Having body confidence means you are more likely to nurture your body than not.

Learning to like what you see in the mirror and wanting to be the best version of *you* (not a clone of a celeb/sportsperson/model/your best mate) is a key part of being healthy. It's what allows you to make smart choices, based on what your body needs.

CONCLUSION

If you are leading a healthy lifestyle, your body is as it is supposed to be, whether you are thin, fat or any of the glorious spectrum of human shapes and sizes that falls in between.

CHAPTER FOUR

1 HATE MY _____

TASH

When I first started writing this chapter, I started subconsciously hashing out all the clichéd bollocks you normally hear about how 'even the hottest superstars hate something about how they look.' If celebrities 'outing' themselves as insecure had a positive impact on the rest of us, *Heat* magazine would have saved the world by now.

Knowing that Cameron Diaz suffers with adult acne or that Robert Pattinson squirms through his A-list life riddled with insecurity about not having a six pack might make you feel better for about five minutes but it's not going to transform how you feel about *your* body. In fact, all the endless whinging celebs do about how they 'hate' this or that can serve to make us mere mortals feel even more inferior – if Angelina Jolie doesn't like what she sees in the mirror, what hope can there possibly be for the rest of us?

So how do we tackle body wobbles? The first thing to know is that it's an ongoing process. Just as nobody wakes up one morning and says, 'Right, from this day forward I have decided to be *really* insecure about how I look,' you don't 'cure' body dissatisfaction in one day and then live happily ever after. Changing what you see involves looking at yourself differently: a habit you learn and then keep practising every time you catch a reflection of yourself in something shiny.

Our perception of our 'flaws' tends to come from two places. First, from our early childhoods: when we're very young, we don't have what is known as 'critical faculty', which is the ability to analyse the things people say to us. We just absorb the world like a sponge, believing everything we are told. So if someone makes an off-the-cuff remark, like 'Oooh, hasn't your nose got big, like your dad's?' or 'What's going on with your hair?' we simply accept there must be something 'wrong' with our nose/hair and start to focus on these things.

This leads to a process known as 'compartmentalisation' and that's the act of looking at tiny chunks of yourself, rather than the whole. When other people look at you, they see all of you at once. They look at your body in the same way they would a table or a tree. When we look at ourselves, our eyes are drawn to whatever we like least and that's what we focus on. Very clever people with brain scanners have actually proven that a completely different part of our brains 'lights up' when we are looking at someone else's body than when we see our own reflection or picture. That means we quite literally see ourselves in a totally different way.

The act of establishing a positive relationship with our body is being able to reverse both of these processes. First of all, try and think where your ideas about how you look and how you should look have come from. Consider that the people you have picked these ideas up from – whether it's friends, family or the media – might not be the most objective. They might have been in a bad mood that day, what they said might have been a reflection of their own insecurity or their ideas about beauty might be incredibly narrow (and, therefore, totally inaccurate).

Try to identify something you like about how you look. Make a conscious effort to switch the focus to these parts when you look in the mirror. After a while, you'll start to see yourself differently.

It's worth noting at this point that, as I work with 500 teenagers a week, I suppose, technically, I must be exposed to a lot of spots/greasy hair/puppy fat. Yet I genuinely don't notice those things about people. Even on the most superficial level, the impression we leave is tied up with things like how we stand and move, how much we smile and how we speak. When people say, 'beauty comes from within,' it isn't as bullshitty as it sounds. If someone gives off a really good vibe, I remember them as being incredible looking because it made me feel good to be around them.

When we're thinking about our 'flaws', we sub-consciously draw attention to them and end up with nervous 'tics', like repeatedly pulling our jumper down to conceal our stomach, for example. We end up drawing attention to the things we like least about ourselves. If you don't act like something's a big deal, no one else will think it is either.

If you're being teased for an aspect of your appearance, know this: bullies target people not because there is anything 'wrong' with them but because they seem like the sort of person who would be bothered. They're looking for a reaction.

Whenever I go on TV, people who disagree with my opinions (and there are lots) flock to Twitter to call me 'fat'. Their logic is, as far as I can work out, 'I don't like what she is saying. She is female and she'll be really upset if I call her fat. This is the easiest way for me to hit her where it hurts.' (These are the same people who, if they agreed with what I was saying, would fill my timeline with compliments about how ravishing I am.) In those situations, I tend to reply with a variation of 'Yep, I am a bit fat. I'm also kind, clever and fucking gorgeous. What's your point?' In most cases that shuts them up.

Loving your body means acknowledging that it isn't

'perfect' but that it's yours, it's the only one you'll get and that you can rock your own brand of gorgeous.

NADZ

I used to HATE, HATE, HATE my boobs; it felt like my body had run off into adulthood while I was still busy being a kid. The developing curves just didn't correlate to the child within. I'd strap them down with layers upon layers of masking tape to try and make myself flatter. I wasn't ready to grow up. But who is? My mum recently told me she still feels sixteen inside. They would make me cry and I felt so much shame at becoming a woman. When I S.L.O.W.L.Y. began to accept that they weren't going anywhere, I began hunting down the right bra, rather than being in denial. I then realised how they could suit my body if I worked with them, rather than against by giving myself four-boob syndrome from attempting to squelch them into an A-cup.

I also used to detest my self-harm scars and, all the way through my twenties, I would create black sleeves that I had cut from tights and wear like long gloves when it was too scorching hot to wear hoodies.

It was only when I went on holiday to Devon with a group of friends that things started to change. We were at the beach, everyone in bikinis and trunks, me still wearing my sleeves. One of the boys made a joke about how I'd have an uneven tan, prompting one of the girls to ask me what they were. After I semi-explained that there were 'marks' underneath, she simply said, 'Just whip them off, we won't mind. We all have weird stuff too.' Like it was nothing. Yet for years I had carried around the weight of these wounds. While I didn't do it there and then, that little comment stayed with me and soon I experimented by taking them off on nights out when pubs or clubs were dark. If I cared less, other people seemed to as well. Even if they did stare, the fact I was learning to shrug it off is what sang loudest to me. I now realise that these were the baby stepping stones towards accepting myself.

Without being all 'Kumbaya' about it, I now focus on what I *do* have, rather than what I don't. I'm blessed with two arms, two legs, a beating heart and five senses.

Yes, I wear make-up, dye my hair and go to the gym but these things are to celebrate who I am, rather than apologise for it or hide from myself.

CHAPTER FIVE

1 FEEL LIKE I'M DIFFERENT FROM EVERYONE ELSE – HELP!

GRACE

The thing about difference is that, without it, everything is the same. I know that sounds really obvious but seriously – imagine a world where everything is the same.

Imagine a place where every person you meet wears the same stuff, talks about the same things in the same way and likes to do the same activities, eats the same food, listens to the same music, lives in the same houses with exactly the same decor in towns that look the same... I'm pretty sure you got bored reading that because I got bored just writing it. We're humans – we don't want everything around us to be the same. So is it really such a bad thing being different?

It's not usually difference in itself that is the issue.

Normally, when I meet someone in a school who tells me they feel like they're different and it's getting them down, I ask if they feel lonely. Almost always they say yes.

Genuine loneliness is one of the worst things I've ever felt. I don't think that being different is what leaves you lonely though. I think that feeling lonely is about not having a sense of belonging and feeling like you're not connecting to anything or anyone.

What I've found is that, strangely, all the things that I know make me different turned out to be the things that have helped me to connect with people in the most genuine ways, giving me the greatest sense of belonging and zero feelings of loneliness. The turning point came when I learned exactly who I was, what actually set me apart from others, where I could find similarities with other people and how to connect with them, embracing both our similarities and our differences.

For example, I've always known I don't just 'like' music but that I need it to survive. (I'm very aware I sound like an X Factor contestant right now but I can't think how else to say it. Soz.) I've always known that cake makes me incredibly happy, that I will always pick rugby over football, that, if I happen to be in a place foolish enough to play music in earshot, I'll involuntarily bust a groove. But knowing these things didn't mean I knew who I was.

These days, I've worked out who I truly am. So I know that, yes, I need music to survive but I also know that making it the only thing in my world will take the shine off. I know that cake makes me happy but also that it makes me incredibly itchy and agitated (see chapter on skin). I know rugby will always be better than football (and that really is all I have to say about that). I know that, if music is in earshot, I will bust a groove but I don't have to for the entertainment of everyone else.

It's one of the hardest things to do, working out who you are; it takes a long time and, because you're a human, you'll always be evolving, so you'll always be playing catch-up with your own brain too. But knowing yourself makes it easier to notice if you have things in common with other people.

Knowing yourself means that, even when you're totally different from everyone in the room you're in, you don't feel lonely, because you know that your differences aren't a barrier to bonding with others. It also means you have the confidence not to try to 'fit in' or deliberately 'stand out'. You don't have to be a cartoon version of yourself: you can just *be*.

So if you feel like you're different, challenge yourself. Try something for the first time: that might be a new skill, sport, club, visiting a new place or doing something that you'd normally do with a friend by yourself. Even if you're not sure you can do it, have a go.

The point isn't to be good at whatever it is you choose to try, the point is to notice how you feel while it's happening. Did I enjoy the challenge? Why/why not? What would have made that more fun for me? What does that mean? That's how you get to know yourself and you'll probably meet some people you like along the way.

NADZ

Truth is, there will always be someone hotter/smarter/more talented than you, just as you will always be hotter/smarter/more talented than someone else. Once you accept this golden nugget of wisdom, you can understand that you're not superhuman and it's OK to not be exceptional at everything. Only then can you begin to capitalise on your differences, rather than aspiring to 'fit in'.

A strong character and amazing personality are far more impressive than being a flawless sheep. Look at people like Lady Gaga, Russell Brand, Vivienne Westwood, Marilyn Manson – they all took advantage of their eccentricities to be where they are today without bowing to conformity.

Note from Tash: David Bowie! David Bowie! He did that too!

Whenever you feel bad, remember you are the result of four billion years of evolutionary success. That is a siiiick badge of honour. Your individuality is most definitely a blessing, not a curse. Try and take yourself out of the moment and think about what you can work towards. When I was struggling, it was really hard to see beyond that wall of pain. If only I had known that by the age of sixteen, I'd have a really close relationship with my sister. By seventeen, no longer want these bullies as mates. By eighteen, be studying at uni (and making my own money at a bar). At nineteen, have a solid circle of mates. Graduate at twenty-two, with a post-grad a year later. Go on to travel the world, live in LA, interview A-listers and report at the Oscars. Have an editor title at a national newspaper by twenty-nine. And be writing a book in my thirties to help inspire people.

I bid farewell to my teens a while ago now (although may, on occasion – 'all the time', say Tash and Grace – still act like one), yet there are times when I still don't feel right. Buuut, before that depresses you into thinking it will never get better, I hope this proves you are not alone in your thinking, you're certainly not a freak and thinking positively really can help you fight the despair if you have the courage to tackle it.

CHAPTER SIX

WHAT ARE THE CHANCES SOMETHING BAD WILL HAPPEN?

(INCLUDING THOUGHTS ON SELF-HARM)

TASH

Up until we're about twelve years old, if an adult tells us doing something will cause us to burn ourselves/catch a cold, stop or the universe will implode and everyone in it will die, we tend to just say 'Oh, OK then,' and not do it. In our teens, however, our brains are wired to question authority and to take risks. We start thinking things like 'but *why* do I have to...' 'That's not fair though...' and 'Seriously, what's the worst that could happen?' These sorts of questions help us explore who we are and set us on the journey to becoming kick-ass adults with fully evolved brains that don't just mindlessly accept the status quo.

The problem is, of course, that risk taking, as the name implies, isn't always a good thing. There are some life events that are rites of passage (like breaking a curfew or wearing a really ill-advised outfit you will only be able to look back on through your splayed fingers while making a sound like a chinchilla being tortured). Other risks simply aren't worth it because they're a) an indication you're struggling emotionally, b) highly addictive, c) both.

In this next section, Nadz and I discuss the risks that can have long-term implications and how to deal with difficult feelings that make you want to hurt yourself.

Back when I turned sixteen, we didn't have proms. Proms were something only Americans did. Instead, on the last day of our school career, we wrote stuff/drew penises all over each other's uniforms, covered ourselves in silly string, wandered about the school halls saying 'Woo hoo!' and generally really annoyed everyone who wasn't us.

When the historic occasion of my last day of Year 11 arose, I seized upon the idea that the only way to make it as special as it needed to be was to paint my eyelashes with glittery nail polish. Luckily, my friend Lydia found me in the loos just before I was about to apply the polish and explained that, at the very best, I'd lose all my eyelashes and, at worst, I'd get some polish in my eye and go totally blind.

What I wanted, in that moment, was sparkly eyelashes, which I've since learned are entirely possible to achieve with the use of glittery mascara. But at the time, I didn't know glittery mascara existed.

The point I'm trying to make is this – if what you're about to do is really, really stupid, there's nearly always a better way to achieve your goal. The trick, a lot of the time, is identifying what that goal is. If you are tempted to go on a crash diet, for example, and someone asks you why, you'd probably say, 'because I want to lose weight.'

Wanting to lose weight isn't actually in the spectrum of natural human desires (just like 'I feel fat' isn't a real human emotion), so what you need to ask yourself is what you think losing weight will achieve. Is it because you want to be healthier (in which case a crash diet will have the opposite effect), is it because you feel insecure compared to your friends, or because you want some attention?

Almost everyone who kids themselves they are only going to do something once as a short term-fix, whether it's a crash diet, taking drugs or binge drinking, is doing it for a reason that isn't going to go away in a day.

The first time I made myself vomit, I told myself that it was a method of weight control and that I just wouldn't let myself eat that much again, but that I 'needed' to be sick. The question I should have been asking myself was 'Why am I so scared of gaining weight?'

The truth was I was terrified that, if I put on weight, I'd become invisible. So that's why I was prepared to do something as illogical and, let's face it, completely disgusting, as forcing myself to puke.

Our bodies are much cleverer than we give them credit for and they aren't designed to be controlled by the random bonkers diet and exercise plans we dream up in our emotional brain. So, if you make yourself sick once, it is still enough to leave you dehydrated and your body will register that it hasn't been nourished in the way that it expected. It will then release chemicals to try to counteract this – ones that make you *really* hungry. This will result in a compulsion to 'binge' (to eat a large amount of food in a short space of time) and probably feelings of guilt and shame followed by the urge to make yourself sick again. And so the cycle begins.

I remember reading testimonials from people who developed eating disorders and thinking, 'I'd never be that stupid.' I thought I was different, stronger, that I had more willpower and could stop at any time. For eight years I told myself, 'Tomorrow will be different. Tomorrow will be the day I stop doing this,' and that was the most dangerous bit of self-delusion.

If you're even asking yourself 'Can I do this once and get away with it?' you need to ask yourself why you feel the need to do it in the first place. Are you anxious, panicked, lonely or bored? If so, there are a gazillion better, healthier ways to exorcise those emotions. Ones where you get to keep your sanity (and your eyelashes).

NADZ

Just as some peeps sink their weight in Jägerbombs on a Friday night then happily go about their lives the rest of the time, we know that others use alcohol as a crutch to mask their troubles and sink into the depths of addiction. Similarly, with self-harm, people may dabble and conclude 'it's not for me', while others spiral into long-term problems. Experimenting with self-harm will not necessarily lead to a twenty-year habit but, equally, it might. So while self-harming once to figure out for yourself what it's really like might not seem like a big deal, it's the consequence of possible dependency which follows that is.

Trying anything once – whether it be drugs, a threesome, punching a wall in rage – guarantees a 'Sliding Doors' effect and you can never truly know the outcome. We're not psychic (if you are, you should join the Criminal Investigation Department and catch crims). So instead of acting on impulse, consider if you're prepared to face the aftermath of your actions. It's like when a teacher tells you to count to ten before you fight back, which seems the *lamest* advice ever for an angry person but makes it possible to step outside the situation temporarily and think of better ways to react.

The truth is that self-harm is not emo, edgy, nor does it solve issues. It only adds to them by bottling up the real problems. It is lonely, messy and traumatising.

If I'm frustrated or sad, the venomous voice inside

my head hisses at me that a self-harm fix will sort me right out. Yet, if I can find the strength to resist its ugly seduction for a few minutes, I have the skill to assess the repercussions that might follow: depression, permanent scarring, perpetuating a self-destructive cycle, hating the taunting reflection in a dressing-room mirror every time I go shopping, feelings of shame, suppressing emotions rather than dealing with them, possible infection, potential nerve damage, lying to people, stress of covering the wounds (especially in summer, or at weddings and family events), spiralling out of control, guilt, isolation, release of dopamine fuelling the addiction… it becomes clear that self-harm won't actually solve my problems but add to them.

So resisting the urge to try self-harm once is a step in the right direction. But even when that's been mastered, there's still the problem of difficult emotions that are crying out to be dealt with and all you want to do is scream, 'FFS, feelings! JUST FUCK OFF!! Why can't I be ordinary like everyone else?!?'

Annoyingly, there is no escaping the fact that, at times, we will want to release tension, express anger, yell in rage or feel swamped by pain that feels like it's chewing us from the inside out. What is important to know is that this is totally #normal. Just because social media is littered with photos of people having 'the best time *ever*,' seemingly devoid of drama as they relish awesome lives, does not mean their lives are perfect. It's just that a blazing row with their parents or sobbing into their pillow don't make for cute selfies.

The last thing I wanted to hear was 'talk to someone' but, when I eventually did, it felt like a world of sumo-wrestlers had been removed from nesting on my shoulders. And it was confiding in my sister that planted the seeds to recovery. Verbalising feelings took them from inside my head to the outside so I was no longer drowning in shame. You could try taking up a sport, going for a walk, getting bendy with yoga; physical exertion releases endorphins, which are basically nature's anti-depressant, like buzzing your nut off without the Red Bull.

Cry if it makes you feel better and scream if it makes you feel free (in the garden, at an empty chair, at a stuffed toy – Nemo won't mind). Listen to music, go to a gig, sing at the top of your lungs, pogo up and down until you're a sweaty mess. Take a breath. Lots of them. Have a helpline saved in your phone. Create a plan for the future. Do something random, like go to the zoo, look beyond the confines of your bedroom walls and out into the world.

Or invest in a punch bag.

Write your feelings in a diary, a letter or a blog, start a YouTube channel, anything to take the poison from inside to outside. Understand your anger, rather than run from it. Grow, be self-aware, don't be afraid of your insecurities – instead, use them as ammunition to drive you into believing in yourself and accomplish the things you want to achieve.

Don't wait until New Year's Day to kick-start your resolutions.

CHAPTER SEVEN

THINGS NO ONE TELLS YOU ABOUT DRUGS

In this chapter we'll address the three drug-related questions everyone wants to know the answer to (and no one ever tells you because they're too busy saying that, if you so much as look at a poster of Bob Marley smoking a doobie, you'll spontaneously combust and die, then go to hell and have Satan spank you with a giant spliff filled with razor blades for all eternity).

WHAT'S IT LIKE TO TAKE DRUGS?
NADZ

When I was at school, the story of eighteen-year-old Leah Betts hit the headlines after she died from taking ecstasy. She became the poster girl for 'just say no', though it later transpired her death was not directly due to consuming MDMA but water intoxication after drinking seven litres in ninety minutes (three and a half times the amount you're recommended to drink in a whole day), which led to swelling in the brain. At the inquest, it was stated that Leah may have survived if she had not drunk all that water and that the advice, 'if you take E, take water,' had proved fatal because she had taken it to the extreme.

Before I get a backlash of hate mail from the parentals of the world for implying that drugs didn't kill Leah, I should stress I'm definitely not saying, 'Go and get bare mashed on doves, just go easy on the H_2O,' either. What I am suggesting is that Leah's case screams to me that education is crucial in understanding what to do if you dabble with substances and how to cope with your body's reaction, rather than just have someone inanely rant 'drugs are for mugs' at you.

The reality is you will come across drugs at some point in your life (if you haven't already) and it's probably easier to score class-As than it is to buy cigs down the local supermarket in some parts of the world. So instead of the news scaremongering you with before/after photos of meth addicts, while your mates are telling you not to be a killjoy as 'it's fine, you'll be buzzing off your tits,' the right information can help you make wise choices.

I should've campaigned harder for the film *Human Traffic* to be a bonus DVD giveaway with this book, as it will tell you what no textbook has the guts to print.

Not only will a young pill-popping Danny Dyer gurning his chops off be a distraction from homework but it paints a very realistic picture of what drugs do without patronising you – neither celebrating nor demonising them. A bite-size synopsis: what comes up must come down and, for every high, there is a low. It also strips away the myth that only homeless junkies or hot-mess A-listers are affected by narcs by giving a voice to all the ordinary folk in the middle; the curious, the bored, the insecure, the experimenters, the peer-pressured...

So rather than hand you a flyer with the word 'drugs' in a red circle with a line through it, here is what you can expect if you do take them.

Weed

Forget what the movies tell you about weed; being baked doesn't equate to saying, 'Duuuude, I just totally heard God speak to me,' or pissing yourself laughing so much you wee your pants. (Also, FYI, calling them 'marijuana cigarettes' said no one ever. As the media like to.)

Instead, you are much more likely to feel sluggish, like the weight of your body is superglued to the sofa and menial tasks like making a tea feel like you deserve an Olympic medal for getting off your arse and accomplishing them. Your drug-induced comedic flair won't transform you into the next Jimmy Carr but you'll more likely have your eyes hypnotised to the telly as you watch documentaries about birds of prey or how the Egyptian pyramids got there. You might feel inspired, like you can take over the world; equally, you may feel apathetic, with thoughts cloudier than, err, a cloud.

Regardless, music will sound *amazing*: like you have a sixth sense. Your speech may slow and be hard to get out, so you'll probably feel paranoid about how you soooouuuuuunnnnnndddd. You could vomit, feel nauseous and 'whitey' (when blood drains out of the capillaries under your skin due to a decrease in blood pressure and you resemble Casper). Be prepared for your mates to call you a lightweight… though they're likely to be less piss-takey if you volunteer to do the 'munchies run'.

Amphetamines

Amphetamines, like cocaine and ecstasy, will make you feel what leaflets would call 'euphoric'. In normal speak, this means 'high as a fucking kite.' Nothing will happen immediately and you'll wonder if you should take some more. Don't. Just as you're debating this with friends, your skin will kind of come alive and feel tingly. You might feel a lift in the pit of your stomach, a bungee jump of insides. You're coming up. You'll grow chattier, inexplicably happier, be fizzing with energy. Your problems will evaporate. You will likely be beaming. Whatever is happening in the room will feel like everything.

You will probably want to dance, or tell your life story, or get 'the greed' for more drugs – or all three. You will feel like you love everyone and may feel the urge to text your mum/dad/cousin-twice-removed to tell them you adore them (even if it's 5.30am). Don't. Your heart will be pumping like you're about to skydive (no nice way to say this, your arteries are spasming) and your jaw may take on a life of its own as you grind your teeth in ways you didn't even know you could (unconscious contraction of muscles).

Hallucinogens

Hallucinogens, like ketamine, magic mushrooms and acid, are a whole different game and will take you to a different place. Like, really different. Outside of your own mind different. They will affect the way you judge time and space, guaranteed to leave you confused. These more hardcore experiences consequently lead to tripping, although it's impossible to predict whether it will be a good or bad trip. For example, ketamine may have you giggling in a room full of friends, feeling invincible from the worries of the world. It could, however, leave you feeling surreal, swaying like you're on a ship in the middle of the sea. It could also leave you hysterical in a toilet as the four walls close in on you, convinced life now exists only in that 35cm × 85cm place. This is a K-hole.

Acid lasts for what seems like forever and you could

still be seeing the wallpaper design wriggle like worms twenty-four hours later. Or the poster of Kurt Cobain repeatedly winking at you as Mum comes into your bedroom to ask how the night before went. Reality caves in, life is not as you know it and your brain is overwhelmed by thoughts that become the universe.

This is likely to go on for hours. So repeat the above paragraphs until sunrise.

'Legal' Highs

Legal highs will simulate all of the above, but know that, just because something is 'legal' or sold over the counter/online, it does not mean it is safe (this goes for diet pills too). They are not government approved; instead, stimulants like 'Herbal Haze' and 'Snow White' are made faster than the law can ban them. By the time they are banned, chemists are already creating new ones to replace what can no longer be stocked legally and so the cycle continues. These products have not been tested on anyone or anything – you are the test.

Comedowns

Sounding not too bad? Let's talk comedowns. The comedown strikes as the drugs start to wear off. Suddenly, the friend-of-a-friend-of-a-friend who you've just declared your undying love to and agreed to get matching tattoos with next Saturday is just another stranger. Profound statements like, 'I can feel the yellow of the sun in my heart,' are just dumb drivel. And having sex with your newly discovered 'soul mate' is just another empty shag.

The surge of confidence you had has metamorphosed into paranoia as you fear everyone was wishing you had shut up hours ago. The feelings of acceptance deviate into crippling bleakness, worse than before you took the drugs. Your social skills have backtracked into mental fragility. You will want to hide behind sunglasses, even if it's pissing with rain or pitch black outside. You'll feel guilty but you won't know why.

The flood of serotonin, which had just made you so chronically cheerful for no reason at all, has abandoned you. The sudden spike now depleted into nothingness. The only remainder is a dull ache in your cheeks from having spent all night maniacally grinning. This uninvited and overwhelming depression can feel really grim, especially as nothing particularly bad has happened, meaning it's hard to explain what is wrong. You will want to sleep forever and you will promise yourself 'never again'.

Obviously, as we can't just press a button to magic our serotonin back, you can replenish what you've lost by eating well, snoozing, watching a comedy marathon, being around people and topping up vitamin C with OJ and foods like bananas, eggs or Marmite (it contains tryptophan, an amino acid, which is one of the building blocks of seratonin).

We all know the consequences of drugs – that you could be dealt a bad batch and drop dead, that they make willies shrivel to tinier than a pea and lead to erectile dysfunction, that they could result in brain damage – but we also all know the dangers of smoking too and 10 million people in the UK still puff daily. As for alcohol...

Death is not tangible, we can't see it, we don't know when it will happen, how it will happen and we think we're invincible from harm. The best thing you can do is know that what might start as fun can affect memory, creativity, alter your character and bring on depression. It doesn't take a rocket scientist to know you also risk addiction. The consequences manifest themselves in complex, dark ways other than death.

Ask yourself why you're doing it, rather than going into it blind and following the crowd (and reread our chapter 'What Are the Chances Something Bad Will Happen?'). If you choose to, make sure someone with you knows exactly what you are taking. Most of all, prepare to be a lab rat because, actually, you can never know what will happen.

WHAT ARE PEOPLE LIKE ON DRUGS?
GRACE

So you know I'm a singer and I've spent a lot of time doing backing vocals with bands, travelling with them and having them as family and best friends rolled into one for months at a time. The music industry is notoriously drug riddled and I'm not about to rewrite that script now. The stories are correct. I've seen all kinds of people put all kinds of things up their noses, in their cigarettes/pens/bongs and drinks (but have, thankfully, not witnessed things being pushed into veins – although I've watched the repercussions).

These are often people I grow to be incredibly fond of. They have kind hearts, some of the best senses of humour I've ever encountered, are intelligent, driven and talented at their best, while depressive, cold, cutting and dark at their worst. Are they like that because they use drugs or do they do drugs because they have this type of personality? That's hard to say.

I'm not going to talk about serious addiction – which I'm sure you've been told a million times over is a very real possibility with any drug – because I don't have experience of that. In fact, I have no experience of taking drugs at all (I have a condition called synaesthesia, meaning I can 'see' sound as colours, so it's trippy enough in my brain already).

The only thing I can really, truthfully tell you without bias or conjecture is what they do to other people and how I feel when I'm in a room with people who are high. I will preface this by saying that everyone is different and will react differently to drugs. There's no point in believing categorically that x, y or z drug will make you behave in any of the ways I explain here –

although there are patterns. I've been around someone having a terrible time on the same drug that somebody else is apparently enjoying and I think it's important to always bear that in mind.

People on drugs tend, to me, to seem like a looser or more energised version of themselves, depending on what they have taken. Having said that, they might lose all sense of responsibility, personal space, time, expectations or all of the above. Sometimes, they also lose the ability to walk and talk effectively – which is always 'fun' if you're the only sober one in the room.

I have rarely been around people who become overly aggressive or overly sexualised, although I have seen that a few times and, on each occasion, that seemed to be a real contrast to the non-drug fuelled behaviour of the person in question. I have never felt as though I was in danger around anyone who is high but almost always feel a bit irritated by them.

A lot of the time, the person on drugs is talking too loudly and far too close to me (and I'm tactile and cool with close encounters with almost everyone, so if I'm saying they're too close, they're really invading my personal space).

Note from Tash: Grace and I quite often do 'eye snogs' (where we try and look into each other's brains by touching our eyes together – it's more fun than it sounds). So if Grace says someone is 'invading my personal space,' they are probably humping her.

Either that or they're unable to listen to what anyone else has to say, so are basically having a conversation with their self. They might be chewing their own face a lot – which is a bit grim to look at – or vegging in a corner, completely expressionless, like a mannequin.

The one thing I would say, though, is that I never feel like I've understood more about someone or had a better time with any of my friends because they're under the influence. It's a myth that drugs help you form 'better connections' – it might feel like that at the time but, in reality, you're just chatting shit, convinced that this is the best conversation EVA.

People on drugs are, in short, a slightly different version of themselves and, in my opinion, not a better one. If you want to try things, do it in as safe a way as possible (and only ever because you genuinely want to) but I'd suggest not being under the illusion that you're any more fun or bring anything better to the table solely because you're high.

WHY DO PEOPLE TAKE DRUGS?
TASH

There are two mainstream theories as to why people take drugs – traditionalists maintain that some people have a defect of character that makes them weak willed, that they aren't as 'good' as the rest of us and that, therefore, they cannot resist temptations. They will tell you that addicts have a responsibility to help themselves and that anyone could remain sober if they wanted it enough. (It should be noted that these people have usually never taken drugs.) Liberals, conversely, will remind you that most drugs are highly addictive, whether physically or mentally, and, therefore, *anyone* who had a sniff of a crack pipe, regardless of character, would probably become addicted in a kind of 'it could happen to any of us' way.

If you're interested in my opinion (because I have one, natch), I actually think both of these theories are largely drivel. I believe people take drugs for the same reason people drink, over-eat, self-harm, smoke or starve themselves – all are a way of temporarily escaping whatever is going on in the mind, and all harm us physically. Interestingly, only one is illegal.

Our circumstances play a huge part in shaping our mindset, which is why drug addiction is more common among people who are poor, homeless, abused or have mental-health issues. Drugs are a way of escaping from our cage, whether that cage is within us – a loneliness or anxiety that feels like a constant, exhausting battle – or outside of us, like the realities of living in poverty or coming from a violent home.

Taking drugs is not a logical thing to do. Drugs always come with a risk, whether that's the risk of ingesting a bad batch, the risk of having a bad trip, the risk of doing something completely stupid while under the influence or the risk of becoming addicted. It therefore follows that people who take drugs, for whatever reason, consider that risk worth taking. They are usually either trying to escape something or find something.

Most people have tried weed once or twice. Even your parents. But when drug use becomes a regular thing, involving class-As, there is usually some desperation involved. People who are desperate hardly ever want to admit it and often become quite defensive if you confront them. We have a need as humans to make out like we're 'in control', even when all the evidence would suggest otherwise. There are those that will tell you they habitually take drugs just to 'have a good time' or to 'expand their minds' and it's no big deal. To those people, I would say, if you were already having a 'good time', you wouldn't need to take them. If life was perfect – if human beings were content and happy in every way – the drug trade would not exist.

Equally, 'expanding the mind' can be done in other, less risky ways. There is, according to ex-addict Russell Brand, a moment when you're on acid when you look in the mirror and you realise that the person you're staring at isn't actually you. You see that you are 'the consciousness behind the man' (slash woman) and that you are operating your body but you and your body are not the same thing.

I had that very same revelation aged seventeen. I was listening to 'Sweet Thing' by David Bowie at ear-bleeding volume, lying on my bedroom floor in the shape of a starfish with those giant headphones on that look like earmuffs, gazing out at the star-strewn night sky through the open window. I thought, 'If such raw, untarnished amazingness exists in the world, I must be more than my body.' I was on nothing stronger than the Diet Coke I'd just drunk. Grace tells me she realised the 'we are not our bodies' thing when she was playing sport and saw that her performance on the pitch was determined by her frame of mind. So there are other ways you can 'expand consciousness' (meditation's apparently a good one too).

In terms of drug addiction, I'd argue that it's the responsibility of the whole of society to look after vulnerable people to the best of our ability and then ourselves to build the inner resources that will allow us to be happy. I believe drug addiction is an illness, not a crime and that putting people in prison for possession, to make their lives even bleaker (and in a place where drugs are often rife) is about the stupidest solution there is. But that's because I'm a bleeding-heart leftie liberal and there are plenty of people who disagree with me.

I don't judge people who take drugs and I don't think drugs are inherently evil – I just know that they're unregulated and tend to be taken by people who are, for whatever reason, not in a great place. That's what makes them dangerous and that's why they should always be approached with caution.

CHAPTER EIGHT

WHAT'S THE DIFFERENCE BETWEEN PORN AND REAL SEX?

TASH

Here is what happens in most mainstream porn videos:

Girl is wearing short skirt/cleavage exposing top. Man assumes this indicates she is definitely up for sex. She is absolutely delighted by his assumption and immediately starts masturbating to demonstrate her delight.*

Girl removes clothes. She is completely smooth, hairless, with totally spherical, plastic looking breasts, a completely flat stomach and no cellulite, like some sort of sex-robot. Man plays with her boobs for a bit, then makes half-arsed attempt at going down on her. She wiggles and moans with pleasure, despite the fact that what he is doing wouldn't arouse a dog on heat.

Man produces his penis, with a self-congratulating

flourish. It is already rock hard and big enough to fill a wardrobe. Girl doesn't seem worried by this but, instead, immediately drops to her knees and starts performing oral sex on the mammoth penis. She is somehow able to do this while making eye contact with him and fitting the whole thing in her mouth without spewing everywhere. This all goes on for a disproportionately long amount of time, incorporating various camera angles.

Man suddenly becomes bored with blowjob. He pulls the girl up by her hair, arranges her belly-down and bottom-up on a nearby sofa and starts hammering away at her vagina.

After about thirty seconds, without any preamble, he then puts his penis up her bum. She's really chuffed about this, acting as though this is what she was after all along.

Man continues to, essentially, masturbate inside girl's bum like some kind of jackrabbit. Just before he comes, he pulls his penis out, turns her around and squirts semen all over her face. She is, *of course*, really happy about this.

THE END.

*NB for non-niche gay porn, the narrative is broadly similar, with different outfits.

This is what would happen in real life:

Man says, 'I assume, since you're wearing a short skirt, you want to have sex with me?'

Girl tells him to fuck off.

THE END.

Just as those driving games you find at service stations/in video arcades can't prepare you for the actual act of controlling a car, porn is about as far away from the sort of sex you have in real life as it's possible to be. The people who make porn films would argue that their audience know this and that what they are making is obviously fantasy, in the same way that video games are.

There's a vast difference between what we fantasise about and what we want to do in reality. Porn is designed to be appealing to a completely different part of your brain than the one you use when you're getting down and dirty in your actual bedroom (or wherever).

The problem is that a lot of (in particular) teenage boys claim to use porn to 'learn' about sex. Which is a bit like watching a Disney film to learn how to be a talking lion.

Here are a few things you need to know about porn and real sex:

A lot happens off-camera in porn, like the application of lubricant (it's never easy to put a penis in a bum hole).

Not everyone enjoys anal sex. In fact, I'd go so far as to say few women do. If you want to try it, it should involve a lengthy discussion beforehand. If someone tries to put their penis in your bum without asking, you are well within your rights to slap them/tell them to get that thing out of your face and away from your bum forevermore/throw them out (of your house. Not your bum. Well, maybe both actually).

Most of the men in porn have taken Viagra or some kind of 'performance-enhancing drug' beforehand. Most blokes kind of fluctuate in hardness throughout the act and can't do high-octane thrusting for ages without knackering themselves out.

Porn actors aren't actually enjoying themselves – they are, as their job title would suggest, acting.

Porn is highly addictive and the more you watch, the more extreme the sex acts have to become in order for you to get the same 'high'. There's some *really* messed up stuff out there on the Net for that very reason.

Watching too much porn can actually stop you from being able to 'perform' in real sex situations, thus rendering the whole 'learning' excuse rather counter-productive.

The average penis is between 5 and 6 inches long when erect but they can vary massively.

It *really* is not size that matters but what you do with it that counts. Most of the pleasure-giving nerve-endings in the vagina are within the first couple of centimetres of the opening so, if you can reach them, you're sorted. (Ditto a man's 'g-spot', which is only a couple of inches along the anal wall).

Trying to ejaculate on someone's face is really tricky

in reality and getting semen in your eye stings like fuck (trust me on this one).

Most women don't orgasm through penetration alone and need other stuff involving hands, mouths and, you know, actually being respected and not treated like a piece of sexual meat.

There's no 'right' or 'wrong' way to have sex (unless you're trying to stick it in their ear). Everyone is different and making it pleasurable for both parties takes patience and practice.

Sometimes, the practising is the best part.

CHAPTER NINE

SEXTING... GOOD IDEA?

GRACE

I can't tell you the number of tweets and emails we get from people freaking out about 'revenge porn'. This is when you've sent a private selfie and the lucky person whose phone it has landed in decides to screw you over by showing it to the world.

Everyone I've spoken to – both students and friends – who have had this done to them list the same feelings. They feel hurt and betrayed, embarrassed, upset and, most of all, they feel really stupid.

First, I'd like to tell you this: if you do find yourself in that situation, you're not stupid at all. Trust, a moment of weakness or a desire to feel wanted are probably at the root of sending a snap like that to someone. None of those things are stupid but they are worth thinking about.

If you send a naked picture to someone, you are completely trusting that, whatever happens between the two of you in future, they are the kind of person who won't show anyone else. It's amazing how a break-up can completely transform someone's character. You have to be sure that their post-split hatred for you, a desire for attention or even the bribe of money won't sway them – this is the gamble you're taking.

I guess you've seen Kim Kardashian, ex-*TOWIE* star Lauren Goodger, Tulisa and countless other celebs be subjected to revenge porn. I don't think any of these women are stupid but I do think they didn't consider how their lives might turn out. Suddenly, there's a huge pay cheque on offer for anyone with compromising shots or videos of them. There is no way of knowing how things will pan out so, in a way, you're trusting fate too. It's also worth remembering that a celeb's experience of revenge porn is very different from your average person's. Kim, Tulisa, etc. have huge bodyguards who will elbow anyone in the face if they screw them over, should they need to. And it isn't the famous people of this world who'll have to put up with being ridiculed and bullied in the school corridor, or have no one want to hang out with them at the weekend. Revenge porn is also unlikely to help your career in the way it did Kimmy. In fact, it could actually stop you getting a job but more on that later.

It's also worth thinking about why the person who's

asked for the pic or vid is asking. Is it because they haven't seen you for a long time and they miss you? Absence makes the heart grow fonder and probably makes the horn grow larger... there's something kinda flattering about that and it makes us feel wanted. But them being able to wait would show respect, right? Is it because they're trying to work out whether you're ready to be physical? A conversation would help them do that much more effectively, no?

I'm open to the fact that I might not have thought of all the options and every situation will vary but I would say that it's really important to think – a lot – before you send someone something that personal. Anything you send via text or on the Internet leaves a permanent digital footprint that can never truly be erased. That's a big price to pay for one ill-advised moment of, 'Oh, go on then.'

If someone doesn't want you to think long about whether or not you should do something, it probably means they know you really don't want to do it – their intentions are off. Take some time to assess the situation and trust your gut; it will find a way to tell you if the situation is wrong.

I know you have probably been lectured on the legal implications of sexting already (and found it deeply irrelevant and boring) but it's worth reiterating here as an extra consideration. If pictures or footage that are considered 'inappropriate' of you find their way online, potential employers will probably find them (most companies now carry out searches of job applicants backgrounds because so many people are so well qualified on paper). Not only could sexting affect your chances of getting a job, we have spoken to teenagers who now have a criminal record because of it. If you send a naked snap of yourself and you are underage, or you receive one and show it to other people, this is classed as 'distribution of child pornography.' This might not seem fair (because it isn't, actually) but, the way the law stands at the moment, this is a potential consequence you face.

I don't say any of this to frighten you or to discourage you from sexting. If it's what you really want to do, that's your choice. But all of the stuff above takes a while to think through before you press a button that, in one millisecond, might change your life forever.

Note from Nadz: Remember, 'I promise I won't show a soul' is just another way of saying, 'I want to wank over you.' (And never forget, in the heat of the moment, that person vowing to love you forever can easily screenshot your naked Snapchat.)

CHAPTER TEN

SKIN

GRACE

Having bad skin sucks. Let's not try to pretend otherwise. But having rubbish skin myself has taught me how to be confident in the (spotty-flaky) face of adversity.

I know it's crazily difficult to be full of joy when you know you don't look your best, or even yourself. It has you feeling uncomfortable in your own skin (literally) and it occupies your brain more than most people could believe is possible. But the only alternative to learning to live with it (for a little while, at least) is letting yourself disappear behind it. That's a pretty shitty alternative so... confidence first, solutions later.

CONFIDENCE

You know that moment when you're kind of asleep but starting to wake up? The moment where you can feel whether it's a sunny day or it's chucking it down with rain before you've even opened your eyes. Well, in that moment, every single morning since the age of about twelve (I'm twenty-five now... so... *ages*), I slowly pull my hand out from its cosy place under my pillow and reach for my face. I feel the skin around my chin, both above and below my lips. This is the skin which, if I let it, could have the power to define what my day would be like.

'Flaky' days used to have me terrified of hugging (never mind kissing) anyone. Who wants my dry skin left on their blazer after a warm embrace?! 'Red and angry' days meant talking to myself constantly: 'Don't scratch, don't rub, do we need more tissue? Is it weeping? Can everyone see?' And 'all cracked up' days meant that eating and smiling were going to be absolute torture: 'I'd rather not rip the skin on my face so I'll probably just give laughing at your joke – along with breakfast, lunch and dinner – a miss, thanks.'

Even now, there's no denying that whatever I find in that moment has an impact on how my day pans out – but, mostly, it's knock-on effect dictates what I pack in my bag for the day and the food I choose to eat, rather than how I'll interact with other humans or the conversations I have in my own head.

That was the first change I made: the things that went on in my head. I used to let my thoughts run wild about what other people would think when they saw me and all the wonderful things I could or would do if my skin was fixed. That was probably the stupidest thing I could do. The truth is that I have no idea what anyone else is thinking and I never will.

Worrying is your worst enemy because, if your skin's bad (oh, world, why must you be so cruel), worry and stress is going to make it worse.

You need be a Zen warrior – easier said than done though, right? Well, here's a tip: you can break the worry habit just like you can break any other habit. That's what I did. Any time you have a thought pop into your head surrounding negative skin stuff (or anything negative actually), HALT! Stop the thought dead in its tracks and then list three things you like about yourself. You might have to think really hard at first – because you're in a negative mindset – but soon, they'll come flooding in.

In a few months' time, you'll have broken the habit and you won't worry so much about what other people think – bad skin, great skin or otherwise.

All those ideas about how my life would be different if my skin were better – I was kidding myself. The reason I wasn't connecting with people the way I wanted to wasn't because I had funky skin. It was because I was nervous, negative and squashing myself.

Push yourself a little, be bold, talk to new people, grab challenges even when you're absolutely bricking it. Having achieved something new that day will help to make you feel good and give you reasons to feel (and keep feeling) confident. It'll prove that your skin isn't a barrier. Remember what Tash said about people leaving lasting impressions on others because of their character, not because of how they look. People notice the sparkle in your eyes, the way you walk and your energy in a room long before they notice your skin, no matter how glaringly obvious it is to you.

SOLUTIONS

Once I felt ballsy enough, I went to the doctor about my skin. I told him how I couldn't eat or smile or laugh because the eczema on my face was so sore. He sarcastically chimed back, 'Oh no, is it ruining your beauty?' (Cheers, mate, real helpful, that). But I understood, he probably had lots of other things to deal with, people who were 'actually sick' and maybe me not being able to be the kind of person I am (one that eats and laughs *a lot*) was top of his priority list.

But it was top of mine. So I looked everywhere for other solutions and eventually went to a Chinese medicine specialist who helped me understand the importance of figuring out the cause of my eczema and (by that point) acne. They explained that there could be a million reasons, different for every person, and that treating just my eczema or acne with lotions and potions wasn't going to help me fix it.

For me, the cause turned out to be certain foods. It turned out that eating a vegan diet (nothing that once belonged to an animal) was better for my body, but becoming vegan won't necessarily have that effect on everyone.

I took on a new diet carefully, making sure I still got all the nutrients I needed, just in a way that worked better for me. Fact: everyone needs carbohydrates, fats and proteins. After being vegan for eighteen months (and clear-skinned for about a year), I started to eat meat (in moderation) and fish again. I still stay clear of dairy (as I found out I'm actually allergic to it).

Like I said, everyone is different and not everyone should be a vegan or cut out any food groups – but I think most human bodies work best when they're given the right fuel. So you could start by eating incredible amounts of fruit and vegetables, loads of water and keeping everything as natural as possible. Cook – so you know what's in your food (Mum and Dad will probably thank you for it too) – and sleep enough (skin cells repair and grow at night so, if you're not sleeping, they don't have the chance to fix themselves). Then you'll have a fighting chance of getting your skin to level out.

I'm sure you've been told that spots and other skin conditions can appear because of hormone changes but, more often than not, they are also a reaction to something inside or outside that your body doesn't like – it just happens to be showing up on your skin.

So, I've mentioned the inside but what about the outside?

In my experience (and I'm confident I've tried every single moisturiser/cleanser/toner/spot treatment/miracle skin cure that I can afford – and even ones I couldn't really), natural is best. Even when it comes to acne: I tried to zap mine away with over-the-counter and prescription chemicals and my spots got worse, or only got better until I stopped with the medicine. I also figure that the fewer ingredients there are in your products or routine, the less there is that you could react to.

Also, most of the time, natural stuff is cheaper and (if you feel like it) you can make your own. If you do, you know it's cruelty-free (no animal testing) and you know there are no chemicals. If you're not into making your own stuff but you'd like to learn about your skin and what it needs, find Caroline Hirons (more info in the back of the book), who is my personal favourite blogger/skincare expert. She's honest, to the point and has been working with skin for years. She has specific sections of her blog where she talks about things that work for teens too. Sam Farmer has also made a range of skin care perfect for young skin (boys and girls). It's not all natural but it is raved about by dermatologists, so check him out too!

There are some great recipes online for cleansers you can make out of porridge oats, plant oils or honey and lemon, depending on your skin type. Oats are hydrating (so good for *all* skin) and plant oils are actually a really great thing to cleanse with for dry, sensitive or even greasy and spot-prone skin. I know that sounds insane but acne happens because your body is producing too much oil. This can be for a number of reasons, one of which may be because the thing you're washing with is stripping your skin of it's natural oils, so it's making loads more to compensate. Washing with plant oils will mean your skin doesn't try to make extra oil. Also, most plant oils *will not* clog pores, so no spots! Mineral oils can clog pores though, so be more careful with them (p.s. they're in lots and lots of fancy-schmancy beauty products these days). There's lots of info online if you look for the 'oil-cleansing technique' but, as a rough guide, here's what you need to do:

1. Work out which oil is best for your skin type – avocado, argan or apricot kernel oils will be good if you have really dry skin. Hazelnut or sunflower oils are great if you have acne (add a squeeze of raw honey and a dash of lemon too if your acne's more aggressive). You can find this stuff in the supermarket or health-food shops.
2. Get hold of a few flannels. You want one for each day so there's no time for bacteria to

breed on there – eeww! Seven as a minimum – I have a few more so I don't have to keep on top of washing one a day.

3. Put a few drops in your hands and rub onto dry skin (no water yet). Massage the oil into your skin for at least a minute (massaging is *really* good for your skin and, if you're removing makeup, you want to make sure you get it all. Oil is drawn to oil, so this will take off long-wear foundations and mascara easily if you're thorough).

4. Run the tap to get the water nice and warm (almost hot but not so hot you can't touch it) and dunk the flannel in. Wring out the extra water then put the flannel on top of your face, press it onto the skin and then wipe away the oil. Moisturise and you're done!

CONCLUSION

In short, looking after your skin is important. It's the largest organ your body has. It's your first line of defence when it comes to bacteria and the things you use on it can find their way into your bloodstream.

BUT...

You are not your skin. It may pass, it may not, so please don't wait for spots to vanish or cracks to heal before you work on letting yourself shine through.

CHAPTER ELEVEN

WHAT'S THE BEST WAY TO HANDLE BULLIES?

NADZ

Being bullied is probably one of the loneliest feelings on the planet. It can also be as random as fuck. It often drops out of nowhere and you're left wondering, 'But what did I even do?'

The first thing to know is you are *not* weak. The second is you are *not* unlikeable. And – for the hat-trick – you are *not* alone.

Victims often feel powerless and like there is no way of winning. If you tell, people might think you're a grass. If you don't, will it ever end? Not only this but some people trivialise bullying as 'just part of growing up.' Oh, right. So is inventing illnesses to avoid school just part of growing up too? Or having to deactivate social-media accounts so trolls can't worm their way into your bedroom via cyberspace? Or wanting to self-harm, not eat, get drunk, run away, have suicidal thoughts because self-esteem is so cripplingly low? Is that 'just part of growing up'? Besides, if we're using that logic, surely an overshadowing philosophy should be that kindness is 'just part of being human.'

One of the best tools you can equip yourself with when it comes to bullying is to know that, even if bullies seem aggressive and loud, they are likely to be battling their own silent feelings of shame. To project their self-loathing onto someone else means not having to face their own demons and, more importantly, distracts classmates from seeing the bully's weaknesses. When I started being bullied in Year 7 I was pretty shy, which made me an easy target as I never bit back. But also, the ringleader's dad was very sick. Only looking back now can I see that she was struggling with her own head mess. Picking on someone else most likely gave her a feeling of power when she felt so powerless at home.

In terms of how to deal with it, you could try asking to speak to the bully in private. If not surrounded by sidekicks, they won't have an audience to show-off to. You might say, 'Calling me names is a waste of time, as I don't care what you think of me. If you want to talk about why you do it, I'll be here for you as a friend.' It might surprise the bully that you're standing up for yourself and not going to take crap from them. They may respect your assertiveness – after all, it's pointless for a bully to carry on attacking you if you're not upset by their actions, as they lose out on the dominant role they are hungry for. It's also mature, bouncing the question back to them to try to get to the root of the problem. You could always text, DM or email if you feel uncomfortable saying this face to face.

Another method you could try is, essentially, a physical version of what is written above, without having to say it verbally. So instead of taking the bully to one side, use the confrontation tactics in the way that you carry yourself. Never underestimate the power of body language. If you walk with your shoulders back and head held high, the bullies can see you're not affected by their comments and are likely to get bored if no one is reacting to them. If you walk with shoulders slumped and with your head lowered, bullies see this as insecure. Stride with purpose: it's like fighting back without throwing a punch. It may sound silly but practice in your room, so it feels natural when you're actually on school grounds. A strong footstep will make you look like their equal and they will respect that.

If you feel like you really cannot cope, or if the bullying has turned physical, confide in a parent, teacher or sibling. While it may feel intimidating at first, a problem shared really is a problem halved and a huge weight off your shoulders (remember the world of sumo-wrestlers?)

You could always write your parents or teacher a

letter if you are struggling to find the right words or are afraid of crying in front them. Telling someone can help you get the right support and advice on the best step to take next. It is a big misconception that talking to someone is weak; if anything, it is probably one of the strongest things you can do. Asking for help is part of being alive, whether you're a new mum with a baby, starting a new job in an office of trained colleagues, lost and asking a stranger for directions, or being bullied and simply don't know what to do.

If the bullying is verbal, or the really subtle type where you are left thinking, 'Did that really happen?' keep a diary. Write down all the incidents – exactly what happened and how it made you feel. That way, you have evidence because sometimes it's really hard to articulate what a bully has actually done.

Eventually, when I began to care less about the bullies, they started bullying me less. My only regret was that I didn't try the method earlier. I found strength in music, building a relationship with my older sister, finding friends outside school. I took my focus away from the playground and into the world beyond.

Finding escapism in music and obsessed by going to gigs, I began to phone around music record labels to say I was writing a fanzine for their band, then asked to be put on the guest list. I started going to shows, meeting artists backstage, writing up the interviews. I found a purpose and it wasn't to impress others.

While my classmates were all trying to impress the bully and picking on other people, I got a head-start in life (and happiness) by paving the path for a career outside school. I was doing things, being creative, concentrating on myself instead of my tormentors. And the moment I truly thought about it, I realised I didn't actually want these bullies as friends – why would anyone want to be mates with people who entertain themselves by attacking others? I vowed I would not let them break me. When they saw I didn't care, they backed off. They were surprised by me. Some even tried befriending me again.

My advice? Stand up for what you believe in, even if you are standing alone. And remember, try not to worry about the haters – their opinions won't pay your bills in future.

CHAPTER TWELVE

'MY SCHOOL WON'T LET ME _____. IS THAT FAIR?

TASH

Unless the thing in question is something physically dangerous (like 'set fire to myself'), morally questionable (like 'have an orgy in the middle of assembly'), or will distract you from your studies (like 'come in with a baby poodle strapped to my face'), the answer is probably 'No, it's not fair.' However, sadly, that doesn't automatically mean you get to win.

Schools like to impose rules with absolutely no sensible basis whatsoever, like boys not being able to grow their hair below their collar, or not allowing pupils to wear tights and socks at the same time. This grinds my gears because, if there's one time of your life when you should be able to express yourself freely, it's in your teens.

We have the rest of our lives to 'learn how to be

smart'/wear a suit/be a corporate clone, so why they start us in training for this from the age of five is a complete mystery.

(Largely irrelevant note: I have a friend who does something terribly clever but boring-sounding in London's financial district and she told me that someone in her office was teased for *two years* for coming into the office *once* wearing brown shoes. Two. Years. So there is some truth in what your teachers say about wearing a uniform 'preparing you for the world of work' – if by 'world of work' they mean something lawyery-bankery – but my point is that the 'world of work' should extract the rod from its arse so the rest of us can.)

I can definitely see the point of school uniform, in that it erases wealth difference between pupils, so, in theory, no one is being judged and everyone begins on an equal footing. As someone who didn't have a lot of money growing up, I appreciated that aspect of it, even though my school skirt was virtually floor-length and a really vile shade of brown, meaning everyone in the school looked like a gigantic, floating turd. At least we were all gigantic, floating turds together.

I remember once taking my teachers to task about earrings – we were only allowed to wear ball studs. For the unfamiliar, a ball stud is one of those things that looks a bit like a spot but in silver or gold. (Oh, and it *had* to be silver or gold. There were to be no coloured ball studs of any description. They were ball stud racists.)

Obviously, I could see why my school didn't want us turning up in giant, chandelier earrings in the style of Linda Carter from *EastEnders* that could get caught in something and rip our ears off. But ball studs? Come on! I just couldn't fathom why we couldn't have a lovely stud in the shape of something, like, just to pluck a completely random example out of thin air, the zig-zag stripe painted on David Bowie's face on the album cover for *Aladdin Sane* (it's not that these were the exact earrings I wanted to wear or anything).

So when our SET students ask whether I think it's fair that sixth-form girls are allowed to wear mini-skirts, yet boys have to wear God-awful polyester trouser suits, or that someone got suspended for shaving their head on one side, my instinctual response is 'That's a violation of your, like, *human rights* or something, man! Let's start a mutiny! Who's with me?!'

Unfortunately, this style of approach doesn't get you very far, as I learned to my detriment (my niece is now at the same school I went to and, more than fifteen years after I left, they're *still* only allowed to wear sodding ball studs).

What I have learned through visiting various schools as an adult is that teachers are actually human beings. So, following that, the best way to change something is to think about what you would consider to be persuasive and approach your teachers in that way.

Imagine if someone came marching into your bed-room unannounced, brandishing a petition, going,

'I've put up with you for *way* too long and you *have* to change what you're doing because, *look*, me and all my friends think so.' You'd tell them to shut up and get out. And then probably have a little cry.

Equally, imagine if your teacher is really stressed, marching down the corridor on their way to do something important and someone stops them in their tracks to start rabbiting on about how everything is '*soooo unfair.*' They're far less likely to stop, think and agree without having had the chance to think about what they're being presented with.

If you genuinely think that what you object to has no solid basis, or is a case of gender/race/religious discrimination, the best thing to do is to request a meeting with your Head Teacher/Head of Year. They pretty much have to say yes.

Ask around and see if there are others who agree with you and then get together and compile a clear list of why you think the present rules are unfair and how you would like them to be changed. A face-to-face meeting always works best (because you can do puppy eyes). Yet, if you really can't deal with it, put it all in a letter. *Don't*, whatever you do, start a petition. Some people sign anything just to feel a bit rebellious and your teachers know that.

Above all, try to be grown up about it because teachers just adore it when you're mature (it reflects well on them).

CHAPTER THIRTEEN

WHAT SHOULD I SAY IF I'M WORRIED ABOUT A FRIEND?

NADZ

Sometimes, it's OK to tell someone, 'I don't know how to help.'

If your friend broke their leg, or got the flu, or even had a horrific disease, the rules are fairly clear cut. You know exactly what you have to do in order to be kind: you have to help them get off the bus/bring them chicken soup/visit them in hospital. When they have an illness of their mind, or are hurting themselves, chicken soup isn't going to help. You can ask them how they are but they might not be willing to talk about it or, worse still, you might accidentally say the wrong thing.

It's OK to admit defeat, as there is no textbook with the answers of difficult questions mapped out:

91

Q: Your friend tells you they've stopped eating – what do you do?

A) March them to a doctor.

B) Feed them pie.

C) Run in the opposite direction.

What you could say is, 'I don't know how to help but I'm here for you if you want to cry and I'll try to understand as best I can.' Encouraging your friend to talk to an adult is important and bonus points if you can direct them towards someone who is qualified to know the right thing to say, like a school counsellor. If you don't have one, try suggesting the school nurse, their GP (if they like them) or that they ring a helpline (some useful organisations are listed at the back of this book). This might sound like the *last* thing they want to hear – 'talk to an adult' – especially if they are deep in their melancholy and aren't ready to get better but fixing the issue now prevents a lifetime of fuckery later.

If they start doing things that make you uncom-fortable, like showing you pictures of how they have self-harmed, try to redirect them to talking about how they are feeling and what motivated them to do it. Remember that all of this type of thing is rooted in emotion and you know what it's like to have one of those (unless you are a cyborg) so, however strange and alien their behaviour might seem, to a certain extent, you will be able to understand.

It's also OK to say, 'I'm not sure I'm the best person

to talk to as I'm struggling myself right now, so my head is up my arse.' If being a shoulder to cry on for someone else is distressing, or grinding you down, or feels relentless as nothing you say seems to be helping, it doesn't mean you're selfish or a bad friend.

When I was really sick, a friend of mine cut me out their life. One day, he just told me not to call anymore and that I should get professional help. At the time, I was devastated, abandoned, and thought *he* was the selfish one. Yet, in hindsight, I can see that what I was doing to him was entirely unfair. When he found out that I was self-harming, I felt so relieved that someone finally knew that I began to tell him every time I cut.

I guess I was looking for reassurance; those soothing words that everything was going to be OK. I was craving attention – a personal cheerleader. Yet, no matter what he said to me or how many times he was on the other end of the phone at 3am, I was going to carry on. I left him utterly powerless to help (I'd only tell him after I self-harmed, never before, in case he tried to talk me out of it) and there was no way he could have healed me. He was not only helpless to actually prevent me from hurting myself but he wasn't emotionally mature enough to deal with a mentally unwell person and it wasn't cool of me to put a fellow sixteen-year-old through that while going through their own hormone hell and dealing with their own maze of a teenage brain.

(On a side note, years later, we reconnected and are mates again.)

The crucial thing is to tackle mental-health issues as sensitively and maturely as possible but to also protect yourself. Reassure your friend they are not crazy: everyone has a mental health, just as we all have a physical health – it is most certainly not something only reserved for people with 'issues' or who are frothing at the mouth with zombie eyes and need to be locked in a straitjacket. Nor is it anything to be ashamed of. Make sure your friend has the best chance to nurture their mental health, without sacrificing yours too.

GRACE

I slip in and out of depression. It's happened since I was eighteen but I didn't even know it was depression until about two years ago. I just thought 'Everyone has low moments.'

I also get patches of what I now know is 'mania' – I used to revel in it until I realised I was out of control and wasn't being myself. Once I realised that I was acting out of character (which I probably wouldn't have noticed without some of my closest friends), I started to get help. Strangely, it was when I started to work with the doctors on getting better that I needed to lean on my friends the most, in a way I'd never imagined. All I wanted (all I still want) is for them to help me remind myself of who I am, to let me trust in the information

I'm given from professionals and to help me trust things will work out when I have moments of doubt.

I've realised that one way to help a friend in need more simply is actually not to try to help at all. I don't mean by abandoning them but, in my experience, some people retreat into their shell because they don't know how to be around you and that just makes the situation worse.

Let your friend know you're thinking of them but that you're not trying to fix them. Just saying hi, sending them a joke or telling them about your day will be a great pick-me-up. You might not get anything back at first but it will have made a difference. When I spend time with my friends and we're not talking about what's going on with me, and they're not trying to be my counsellor, I'm able to do the things we normally do. And those are the moments when I feel happiest. The more days like that we have, the more likely I am to open up to them about what's going on and how I feel when I'm truly ready.

In just being a friend, I'm reminded that we have a connection and that I can talk to them, should I wish to. And when I do, what do I want them to say? Not a lot, in all honesty. I just want to know that they are aware of how I feel or of the things I find difficult. I don't want answers from them – that's what my doctor's for. I don't want them to 'cure' me: I'm learning how to do that myself. I just want someone to listen and, if they can see I'm a little bit 'off', to give my hand a squeeze.

Your friend might not be able to tell you for a long time exactly what it is that they want or need from you – I know I couldn't – but making them aware you're available for a chat if they wish can be just as effective as having the chat itself.

TASH

The most helpful thing friends can do, in my opinion, is to watch their language, by which I mean be aware of the words you use when you talk to your mates. Words are really important because we're constantly absorbing them and, even though we might not realise it, they can shape our attitudes and beliefs.

People with low self-esteem need to be reminded regularly why they are valued by the people that love them and that the love they receive is not conditional upon how they look or the grades they receive. We don't love people because they just got an A in their Biology exam and we adore their new trainers, yet, weirdly, things like this are often what we give the most attention to.

When you feel low, you're often left thinking, 'What is the point of me?' We live in a society where we're told that, if we are good looking and wealthy, we will automatically be happy. This is utter bollocks (in reality, chasing these values has made an awful lot of people desperately unhappy – trust us, we work with celebs). But when you are at your lowest ebb, it's easy to cling on to the idea that, if only you looked like a model and owned warehouses full of cash, your problems would disappear. When I had an eating disorder, it was trying to be super thin that was causing my issues and yet, for some reason, I persisted in believing that, if I could only reach my miniscule target weight, it would magically solve them, which kept the whole toxic cycle going. If only someone had found a way to say, 'Actually, no one who matters gives a tiny little rat's arse what you weigh.'

You can help gradually boost your friends' confidence every day by acknowledging when they say something smart, do something brave or when you have enjoyed spending time with them. Try saying things like, 'I appreciated you being there today,' or, 'That was really witty, what you just said.' This is a way of subtly letting your friends know that you think they are awesome, without having to go and find a field somewhere, hold hands and make a caring circle while gazing into each other's eyes and earnestly saying, '*you*, my friend, are awesome,' (which is, let's face it, not #normal).

A lot of people are put off this kind of compliment-giving because you don't tend to hear it in everyday conversation and they think they'll sound like a dick. Fear not! As long as it's an authentic response to the moment, no one will laugh at you – and if they do, it is *they* who are a dick (fact).

If you feel a bit awkward giving compliments face to face, that is precisely why text messages were invented.

CHAPTER FOURTEEN

"HOW DO I KNOW IF I HAVE AN EATING DISORDER?

TASH

Eating should be a fairly straightforward process – like putting fuel in an engine. Unfortunately, people have, over the centuries, found infinite ways to fuck it up.

This, combined with the constant deluge of conflicting information we're exposed to on the subject of diet and exercise, can make just feeding yourself a really confusing process. This explains why I'm asked at least once a week by teens how you know if you have an eating disorder.

My hunch is that they probably suspect that they, or someone they know, is suffering from an eating disorder and want confirmation that they should be concerned. Even just asking the question probably means something has landed on the 'worry radar' – a feeling that should never be ignored.

When you have an eating disorder, deep down, you always kind of know. When I was suffering, other people around me suspected and I fiercely denied it. I even denied it to myself, going on a quest to find some other terrible affliction that was causing my constant flu-like symptoms, dehydration, bad circulation, stomach cramps, hair loss, crumbling teeth and vitamin deficiencies. Yet I always knew really.

What can be really difficult is identifying eating disorders from the outside and this is something even medical professionals struggle with. GPs have what's called 'diagnostic criteria' but, since these include 'cessation of menstruation' (thus excluding all men), they're actively unhelpful, in my opinion. Eating disorders are a mental illness, so trying to measure them by physical criteria is about as scientific as when people claim they can tell whether pregnant women are having a boy or a girl by dangling a necklace over their belly and seeing which way it turns. (Don't get me wrong, there's a time and place for this kind of mildly entertaining voodoo crap but it's not in the doctor surgery.)

I'll try and pour some clarity on the issue and give you an insight into the mind of someone with an eating disorder but please bear in mind that it would be impossible to do this definitively. If you're worried, that's reason enough to seek some help.

In an ideal world, people wouldn't think about eating

at all. They'd instinctually reach for foods with a high nutrient content to nourish their bodies when they felt hungry. Unfortunately, because we are bombarded with imagery and messaging that, on one hand, encourages us to eat for pleasure and, on the other, demonises people who are overweight, most people have lost the ability not to overthink food. In the twenty-first century, this is, sadly, completely normal – the trick is to try to minimise the amount we think about food.

We should eat and exercise to live, not live to eat and exercise. If you feel as though your thoughts and behaviours relating to food and exercise are dominating your thoughts, that's when you're entering into the territory of an eating disorder.

Eating disorders happen in the mind. Even though they might cause you to lose or gain weight, the weight loss or gain is a side effect of the illness. It is possible to have an eating disorder and to technically be a 'healthy' weight. I find it helpful to compare eating disorders with other mental illnesses because they have a lot in common:

Anorexia is probably most like Obsessive Compulsive Disorder (OCD). People with OCD get locked into a pattern of thinking, which then goes on to affect their behaviour. So they might, for example, believe that, if they don't wash their hands, the germs on them will cause them to become sick. So they wash their hands. But the fear of becoming ill doesn't go away. They try to push it to the back of their mind but that makes the thought worse and more insistent. So they wash them again. The thoughts of germs and illness rise up once more and this time they need to wash their hands for longer to make them go away. Before long, they are caught in a cycle of compulsive hand washing.

If we apply this OCD thought processes to food and exercise, that is, essentially, how the mind of someone with anorexia works. People with anorexia think about food all the time. There is a constant and exhausting argument they have with themselves, over and over again, in which they imagine the food they would like to eat and then tell themselves that they cannot have it. They are usually obsessive about what time they eat, weighing and measuring their foods, and how many calories the food contains. It's a myth that anorexia is purely about starvation – it's about controlling food intake and a fear of what will happen if that control is taken away.

The best way to tell if someone is meandering into anorexic territory is to test their response when they are forced to deviate from their diet and exercise routine. Most of us find routines comforting but, if you freak out when your routines are broken, this usually points to an issue. So, for example, there are certain social occasions when it is expected that we will eat and there are times when our plans dictate that we might have to miss a session of exercise. If someone becomes insistent about having 'special' foods, or swerves/interrupts important occasions so they can exercise, they are probably beginning to think in a compulsive way.

Bulimia and compulsive eating are both types of addiction. Compulsive eating isn't the same as comfort eating or pigging out every now and then for fun. People who eat compulsively rarely enjoy eating and they tend to eat quite quickly, without really noticing flavours. For some people, the shame and guilt they feel for overeating leads to the desire to 'purge' (forcing food out of the body) and this is how bulimia begins. Anorexia often segues into compulsive eating or bulimia because depriving the body of nutrients actually causes the urge to binge eat (see 'What Are the Chances Something Bad Will Happen?' chapter for more details on this).

I have actually experienced both anorexia and bulimia, although bulimia invaded my life for a lot longer. I'd be lying if I told you that, at the beginning, my eating disorder wasn't about wanting to be thin. The thing that united all the years I had eating disorders for was the belief that being thin would make my life better (say it with me, people – 'BOLLOCKS!').

Having said that, bulimia doesn't 'work' as a means of weight control long term. I discovered that after a few months. In fact, it is actually impossible to completely purge your body of everything you have eaten. The body always retains more than you are able to rid of.

Purging usually causes initial weight loss but that's

because of dehydration, so the loss is just water. After a while, the body stabilises and that's why the vast majority of people who suffer from bulimia (and they make up almost half of the total number of people who have eating disorders) are either a 'normal' weight or slightly overweight.

Even knowing this, I got to a stage where I couldn't seem to stop the cycle of bingeing and purging, because I was addicted. Bulimia became, for me, like self-harm. I didn't like myself very much at that point in my life, so I punished my body trying to exorcise the demon thoughts in my brain.

Needless to say, it didn't work.

In fact, the only thing that worked, in my case, was reprogramming my world view so that I could bear to inhabit my own head.

There are some personality types who are statistically more prone to eating disorders than others (but that doesn't mean anyone is 'destined' to get one). In my case, I have a chronic dose of perfectionism. I'm incredibly hard on myself when I don't perform to the best of my ability. I have always been this way, ever since I was a tiny child of the 1980s, wearing Day-Glo cycle shorts and slap-on wrist bands (ask your parents), running around with my Cabbage Patch Doll.

Perfectionism is an integral part of my personality (and regularly drives my boyfriend bonks). It will never go away. When people say, 'Eating disorders never leave you,' what they mean is, 'The reasons you get them never leave you.' That's not the same thing. It is possible to recover from eating disorders because, well, TA DAAAAAA! Here I am.

Eating disorders are just habits.* Conquering them involves two things – discovering why you developed the habit in the first place and then finding a better and more effective way of expressing that part of yourself.

* In my opinion, there are people who will disagree. Someone tried to convince me that eating disorders were 'biological' once (what they meant was they believe eating disorders happen in our DNA, not that they're like washing powder). According to the UK's biggest eating-disorder charity, B-eat, there is absolutely no evidence for this. People who don't want to think of eating disorders as a habit are usually in the 'denial' phase. See above.

CHAPTER FIFTEEN

WHAT SHOULD I DO IF I'M BEING COPIED?

NADZ

People say, 'Imitation is the sincerest form of flattery.' Actually, it's one of the most excruciatingly fingernails-on-a-blackboard annoying things that can ever happen. It leaves you wanting to howl, 'GET YOUR OWN IDENTITY!' at the copycat until your vocal cords are rawer than their lack of originality.

Yet the problem is that telling someone to stop copying is trickier than trying to blag a seat on the front row at the Grammys. Individuals don't own the copyright to how they dress, behave or talk. So if a classmate starts replicating your guyliner and skater jeans, or layering vest tops with Thai trousers, or adopting your trademark catchphrase, you don't technically have the right to stop them.

If you are prepared to confront them, you could gently ask them to back off. However, you run the risk of them feigning ignorance, calling you paranoid or saying something to the effect of, 'Chill, we just have similar styles,' (and there's no comeback to that which doesn't make you sound really paranoid, thus proving their point).

Instead, you could suggest going shopping together to steer them in a direction more suited to reflect their own personality. You can also compliment them on their unique traits to make them feel more comfortable in their own skin, or make recommendations that are similar to you, but not a direct mirror image.

Try to see things positively, in that you've got enough swag to inspire the copycat. Also, rather than presume they are insincere, perhaps you *do* genuinely share interests. If you notice them wearing the same band T-shirts, suggest going to a gig together. If they talk about the same movies or start reading the same books, offer a day of sofa-vegging with Netflix. If they start prattling on about fitness, invite them to go skateboarding or swimming together.

When I was in Lower Sixth, a friend of mine began copycatting my self-harm. She'd make surface scratches on her arm, then sit in class with sleeves rolled up and flail her limbs around in front of the teacher. This teacher ended up giving the girl a lot of support and attention, leaving me infuriated. It angered me that she had taken 'my' problem (I realise now that self-harm is not something I own) and trivialised it into something so shamelessly attention-seeking. It felt like *my thing* that she had 'stolen', debased and wasn't even doing 'properly'.

Eventually, once our friendship had fizzled, I wrote her a letter to ask her why she had taken something so painful to me and played with it like a toy. Credit to her, she wrote back and agreed to everything I had said, even thanking me for being honest and making her face the issue. She said that, although she was an attention-seeker, that was a problem in itself. She revealed that it might stem from the fact that she felt she was often overlooked at home in favour of her younger siblings, once her mum had remarried. When she explained her back-story, I understood why she had done what she did. It showed me that copycats are struggling to find their own stamp. And just as the copycats are not unique, neither are the copied.

Another friend battled anorexia in her teens and hated it when people at school skipped meals but would then scoff down their packed lunches behind toilet doors in secret. She thought it belittled the severity of her mental illness. Yet, looking at it objectively, it's innately human to seek approval and want to be liked, so no rationale is spared when it comes to being noticed. Just as I self-harmed, or my friend starved to 'help' our confused minds, the copycat seeks attention as their way of asking for help.

Remember, when someone copies, they are most likely doing it because they've not yet figured out who they are or developed their own style. The silver lining for you is that, because they're still trying to get to know themselves, they'll probably move on from trying to copy you pretty swiftly, experimenting until they finally do discover who they are. Imitating you won't feel right for long, as it's not genuinely them.

We all take inspiration from things we see or hear, people we think are hot, music that motivates, and mould it into an amalgamation we call 'ourselves'. Copycats tend to just focus on one person, instead of a wider pool. It seems poaching from one thing is 'plagiarism' (a term you'll be all too familiar with if you've ever tried to copy and paste your homework from the Internet) but stealing from lots of things is 'research'.

Know that, if someone does try to duplicate you, it does not take away who *you* are. While it may feel like you've given birth to an unwanted twin, you are not 50 per cent of the person you were before. A person's soul resonates from the inside out, so two people in the same clothes will still look very different. Think of a group – say, Little Mix: they can be all styled virtually identically but there are still four very different people shining onstage.

If all else fails, you could sue for identity fraud.

CHAPTER SIXTEEN

BFFs?

TASH

Pretty much every time I go into a school, the teacher will tell me that they have an issue with 'cliques'. Every school does and that's because school itself is an environment conducive to cliquey-ness.

At school, there is really only one type of friend you can have – a *best* friend (this is particularly true of girls). In the periphery of you and your *best* friend, there's an extended crew of people who 'get' you. It's the logical thing – put lots of people together in the same building for an extended period of time and they will gravitate towards a particular 'tribe' based on musical tastes, humour, values, hobbies, etc. But this set-up can make friendships intense.

Being someone's school-based BFF involves spending

all day together so, if there are things that you find irritating about each other, this inevitably leads to the retraction of the 'Best Friend' status and a period of social isolation. This feels like the end of the world because you go from being closer than you ever knew it was possible to be to someone, to sitting on your own at lunch, furiously staring at a sandwich, while they tell their side of the 'falling out' story to everyone in your year (thus ensuring that they hate you too) and you try not to cry.

There was a girl at my school who used to specialise in this sort of behaviour. She had a gang of about five 'Best Friends' and the status of 'BFF' would be given to whoever was 'in favour' that day. Those five used to compete to see who could 'please' her the most, bringing her little gifts and simpering to her every whim. Every so often, she'd decide one of them had fallen out of line and gather the other four around for a bitching session. Which is totally evil.

You'd see it most weeks, heads huddled around this girl in one corner as they dissected the misgivings of whoever was deemed to have transgressed. And the 'Best Friend' who had been cast aside would be sitting alone in the other corner, desperately trying to pretend that the whole undignified situation wasn't happening.

On a slightly tangential note: Once, I got so fed up of seeing this tediously repetitive soap opera unfold before my eyes every single week that I told the ring leader girl in no uncertain terms that she was a total knob head, in front of everyone, during a speech in assembly. (Remember, I had no interest in being popular.)

I didn't think she seemed particularly bothered, although she did look slightly shocked. I just thought I'd verbally bitch-slapped her in the way she deserved and justice had been done.

Ten years later, I bumped into her in a club in London and she (having consumed *far* too many sambucas) pointed at me and said, 'YOU! You used to bully me at school,' (at which point everyone took a sharp intake of breath and looked at me accusingly). I, of course, wanted to wither and disappear in that moment and realised there was nothing I could say because she had obviously meant it – she wasn't trying to be a cow. In fact, she looked a bit traumatised (slash pissed).

Anyway, the thing that would have stopped that whole embarrassing situation from happening would definitely have been if she'd taken me to one side at the time and explained how much I'd upset her. I, being a reasonable human being, would have felt terrible and apologised and explained myself.

So, going back to Nadz' point about bullying, there's a chance that your 'bully' might just be a girl like me who doesn't even know she is doing it.

School makes everything feel more dramatic because it's where you tend to meet all the people in your life to whom you aren't related. Life after school isn't like that, which allows you to have a 'different friends for different activities' policy. So, for example, you might have a mate who is amazing for a night out but, if you had to take them to a family event, you'd be so embarrassed by them that you'd want to eat your own head. Or you might have a friend you can natter away for hours to about a shared passion for World of Warcraft but who you can't imagine having a conversation about anything else with.

I have 'gym friends' (people I chat to in the gym but, literally, never see anywhere else), 'drinks friends' (usually fellow journalists who also have all the opinions in the world, thus ensuring a highly-enjoyable three-hour, wine-fuelled rant-a-thon) and 'work friends' (teachers who I get on with and can discuss how we need to completely revolutionise the education system – a conversation that almost everyone else would find so boring that they'd be tempted the staple their eyelids to a table, just to check they're still alive).

I have friends I could happily live with and friends who are great for the occasional catch-up but who I couldn't spend more than a couple of hours with without being heavily medicated. I have friends who I can call in a crisis and friends who I can call when I want to go and tear up a dance floor somewhere. I have friends I'd trust with my pin number and friends I wouldn't even trust with their own.

My 'best' friends are probably Grace and Nadz

because I love them like sisters and can be completely vulnerable around them but even they annoy the fuck out of me occasionally (sorry, ladies). That's OK because I don't feel the need to see everything in the same way they do, all the time.

The problem with the 'best friends or nothing' approach is that it often involves moulding yourself into a version of you that fits alongside a certain person or into a certain crowd. We do this because we need to have a sense of belonging (goes back to when we lived in actual tribes pre-civilisation as we know it) but it can work to our detriment because we never truly discover who we are or make peace with the fact that we're actually rather complicated (see 'I Feel Like I'm Different' chapter).

You can like heavy metal but feel no desire whatso-ever to dress head to toe in black and have multiple piercings. You can be a vegetarian but not spend your days in a meadow wearing a crown of daisies and playing acoustic guitar. You can like going to the gym but not feel the need to ingratiate yourself into a group of people whose topics of conversation are limited to how much they can bench press while admiring themselves in the mirror. You can care about women's rights and this season's over-the-knee boots simultaneously (and if this applies to you, I strongly recommend picking up a copy of *Cosmo*).

It's also OK to want to spend time on your own. The

most mentally healthy state to be in is one where you are able to be alone and in groups of various sizes at different times without freaking out.

You don't have to conform to a stereotype. Everyone is different from everyone else. We're also fundamentally the same. That's what makes us marvellous.

So I suppose what I'm trying to say is this:

1. You'll only ever really know if your 'BFF' is your BFF after you have left school. If you're currently BFF-less, chatting and bonding to someone else in your school doesn't necessitate having to change your entire personality (you might even enjoy it).

2. If you've never had a BFF, don't fear. There are 7.1 billion people on the planet and an average school contains (*tries and fails to do maths*) a, like, *miniscule* percentage of that.

CHAPTER SEVENTEEN

'EVERYONE'S DOING IT...

GRACE

Picture the scene: I'm twenty and driving through America – LA, to be exact. It's summer, nighttime and I'm in a tour bus (I say bus – I definitely mean nine-seater van), which is packed fit to burst with amps, guitars, leather jackets and too many pairs of Ray-Bans. On board are myself, Lee, Josh, Sam, Frank, Jonny, Chris, Jack and 'The Rogue'. (I actually just sat for five minutes trying to remember his real name, only to realise that I don't think I ever knew it!)

I've known them for two months, they've known each other their whole life and, from the names on that list, you've probably guessed that I'm the only girl. We've just played a show in a canyon in San Diego and the crowd reaction was insane. We're buzzing because

117

America loves their music, the record label are happy and we feel like rock stars. Girls have been throwing themselves at the band, guys have been throwing themselves (in a slightly less obvious manner) at me and we've had loads of free booze.

At the same time, though, I feel a bit lonely. I've only known these people for eight weeks and have only really known which one was which for about two of those weeks if I'm honest (learning eight new names when everyone has five nicknames is really hard). I'm far away from home and they know each other inside out and back to front, not to mention the fact that they ooze cool out of every pore. I want to connect with them and be true to myself, I want them to get to know me so I really, truly feel as though I fit in and I've made lifelong friends but it seems like it's harder for me to click with them than normal. If I'm honest, I'd do almost anything at this point to fit in.

Then someone brings some 'fun dust' to our inside-van party. I'm not into drugs. I have friends who are and that's fine but it's not for me. I'm hyperactive and have a runaway imagination and I don't like the idea of not being in control. So in that moment, my heart sank. I'm already the odd one out and here's a way for me to be on the same page as them but I know I'd have to step off my page to do it. The bag is passed round, offered to me and I say, 'Nah, I'm good thanks.' I don't know if it was fear that stopped me or whether

I suddenly became really ballsy and decided to be true to myself but, either way, I didn't take the baggy and, over the next few weeks and months, the most surprising thing happened.

We ended up touring for a year. Throughout that time we travelled to an insane amount of cities in countries all around the world and we'd meet, say, ten new people that we had to work with every single day. These were the kinds of people who wanted to fit in; people who wanted to impress the band, accommodate the band, bring the party and make sure none of us remembered how tired and far away from home we were. All of them figured out the same thing: drugs are the kind of gift you can bring to a band that makes you look 'cool', not too creepy and will make sure that they party hard.

I worried that I was going to have to turn down drugs every single day and that, because of that, there'd be a daily reminder to all the boys that I was different, not quite as 'cool' and not one of them. That's not quite how it played out though. After about a week or so, the people I spent every day with were all aware that I didn't take drugs. We actually talked about it one night in the van: they said that they noticed but they never felt like I judged them because they did. I explained why I didn't and they completely understood.

From that day on, hardly anyone offered me drugs again. If they occasionally did, one of the boys would jump in before I had to turn them down and say, 'Nah, not for Gracie.' It wasn't an issue. It didn't make me feel separate from them – strangely, it brought us closer. Every single one of them, at one time or another, told me they thought I was awesome because I was always myself. They told me they were able to be themselves around me because they knew that's what I was doing and that, therefore, I wouldn't judge. They even said that me being the one who didn't join in the 'drug party' helped them have a 'day off' if they wanted.

In that year, more than ever, I learned the value of being authentic. Before that moment, they hadn't figured me out, probably because I hadn't shown them anything real. They taught me that respect and attention are not the same thing. In order to gain respect, you have to show that you respect the people you're with and yourself enough to be authentic.

Being yourself will *always* be in fashion and it's not possible for anyone to respect you if they don't know what you stand for. Whatever it might be that everyone's doing and you don't want to, do what you know feels right to you.

You might be surprised at the response you get.

CHAPTER EIGHTEEN

AM I READY FOR SEX?

TASH

The girl who was the first to 'do it' in our school made sure everyone knew about it. It's the same everywhere, I think. Someone is always the first to do the 'dirty deed' and they become a bit God-like for a while because they know something everyone else doesn't.

This particular person came marching in one day in Year 9, all full of her own self-importance, and immediately started whispering to the first person she saw, who then whispered to someone else and, shortly afterwards, she was surrounded by a group of about twenty people, all intently listening to her.

She told us all about the older guy she was seeing (who was, of course, just 'so fit' and amazing) and how they'd progressed from doing 'suck tits' to 'fingering' and how last night they had then done '*it*'. I never cease to be amazed by how many terms we came up with for various things you do during foreplay. Americans have 'bases' – first base being (I think) kissing and fourth base being (again, I think) actual penetration. We, on the other hand, had terms like 'suck tits', which seems a little less sophisticated.

Someone (it could have been me, actually) asked her 'Don't you think you're a bit young?' at which point she announced, 'If you're old enough to bleed, you're old enough to breed,' and dared us all to challenge her. We didn't because what she said had rhymed, so we assumed it must have been true.

That girl was, I now realise, an utter dickhead because, of course, in some countries they abide by the bleeding/breeding rule and force girls to get married as soon as they start their period, often as young as ten years old. These same girls often die in childbirth because their bodies aren't developed enough to be able to cope with 'breeding'. So if you're old enough to 'bleed', you definitely *aren't* automatically old enough to 'breed', even on the most basic physical level.

In fact, sex is one of those instances in life where your body usually races way ahead of your mind. At some point during your teens, you are going to become as horny as fuck. You're going to stare at pictures of celebrities you fancy for hours on end with your mouth open, dribbling slightly. If someone you're attracted to talks to you, it'll feel like an electric shock. You'll start looking at the world around you, trying to identify objects you can rub yourself on that might feel nice.

All of this is totally normal but it doesn't mean that you are ready for sex. Being ready for sex involves asking yourself two questions: a) Am I in the right head space to deal with this? b) Is the person I'm thinking of shagging also in the right head space?

When your mind is being clouded by all the horny, being able to answer the above questions is quite a feat. It's also pretty futile to start asking yourself about 'love' and 'respect' because it's really easy to kid yourself that someone loves and respects you when you fancy them so much that you want to bite them into little chunks, pulverise them into love jam, spread them on toast and eat them.

It's easier to do a checklist of 'warning signs'. These might include:

Am I too embarrassed to seek out contraception?
Am I too embarrassed to have a conversation with the other person about what contraception we're going to use?
If other people find out, would I feel deeply ashamed of them knowing I had sex with that person?
Do I feel too self-conscious to show my naked body to that other person?
Am I doing this out of curiosity?

Am I doing this to prove a point?
Am I doing this because I feel pressured?
Am I in two minds about this decision?

If the answer to any of the above questions is 'yes', you're not ready for sex.

Then ask yourself:

Would I feel comfortable stopping 'proceedings' and asking someone to put on a condom?
Would the person I'm thinking of having sex with support me if something went wrong with the contraception?
Do I trust the person I'm thinking of having sex with not to brag about it?
Do I trust the other person to stop if I ask them to?

If the answer to any of the above questions is 'no', they don't actually love or respect you. Sorry.

Don't read this wrong: I'm all for sex. Sex is awesome. Anyone who tells you different isn't doing it right. But bad sex is definitely worse than no sex and the fastest route to bad sex is to be doing it for the wrong reasons. Even if you're totally inexperienced and have no idea what you're doing, you can still have what I would term 'good' sex if you're able to laugh about it and learn from it. Sex is the establishing of a bond between two people and, when the mind and body work together to establish that bond, that's when sex becomes this awesome experience, rather than just a meaningless bonk.

I'm not against one-night-stands either but respect plays a part in those too – usually respect for yourself. It's important to distinguish between 'sex' and 'attention'. Sometimes, what we really want is to flirt with someone, to feel wanted and like we *could* have sex with them if we chose to. It can feel like the actual having of the *actual* sex is the inevitable consequence of putting yourself in that situation but it really isn't. Putting a piece of your own body inside someone else's, or having someone put a piece of them inside you, is a really intimate thing. I know sometimes it doesn't feel that way because it looks as though everyone is just shagging on a whim whenever they feel like it, but it is.

Sex sells and that's why we live in a world where sex is often presented as the solution to everything; the holy grail that will mean we are suddenly having the time of our lives. The idea of sex has been packaged up and sold back to us so that we'll consume things, whether it's food, films, makeup or box-sets in our quest for it.

The thing I wished I'd known about sex before my first attempt at it was that I really should have been doing it with someone to whom I had the confidence to admit my inexperience. As it was, the other person kind of just presented me their genitals and, having never seen a penis up-close before, I didn't know what

I was supposed to do with it. (I feel really sorry for heterosexual men and lesbians in this regard, as vaginas are much more complicated and diverse than their male counterparts. The best you can hope for is that you're with a girl who has taken the time to discover what she likes and can give you some instructions.) I didn't feel that I could properly inspect the area or, indeed, ask them what they would like me to do. I'm not sure why, looking back. I think I just didn't want to seem stupid. So I ended up ad-libbing, all the time wondering if I was getting it wrong and whether he would laugh about it later. That in itself should have told me that I wasn't with the right person.

Real sex is messy, squelchy, hairy, jiggly and grunty. It isn't *Twilight*, it isn't *Fifty Shades*... and it isn't anything like porn. It's better. If you're ready.

CHAPTER NINETEEN

IF I TELL SOMEONE, WHAT WILL HAPPEN?

NADZ

Sharing a secret can be really daunting, as you're not only revealing something personal but you can't predict how the other person will react. As someone who desperately struggles to articulate my feelings, I'd recommend writing a letter. Putting something on paper means cutting out the latter part of the equation (at least temporarily) and not having to worry about a face-to-face confrontation.

Letters also mean you can write as many drafts as you want until you feel it's right, rather than saying something out loud and it not come out as intended. It also eliminates the risk of being interrupted or shouted at before you get to finish what you want to say by an angry parent who might feel like they have failed.

127

If you feel that your secret might shock or upset the person you're telling, a letter gives them a chance to digest what you've told them in private before speaking with you, so they don't lash out and can think of the best way to give you advice.

When I first told my mum about my self-harm, I made her guess what was wrong with me. I was so ashamed and frightened of how she might react that I felt I couldn't say the words aloud. She had guessed something was up, as I grew more and more withdrawn from life, so one night she came into my room and asked what was going on with me. With the lights off and me under the covers, she sat on the edge of my bed. I lay in dread as she reeled off all sorts of things that might be wrong, from pregnancy to drugs to making myself sick to exam pressure. It felt like an eternity before she finally asked if I was cutting myself.

In that split-second, despite having feared the worst, I was drenched in relief: momentarily weightless. At last, she knew! Afterwards, she told my dad for me. Don't get me wrong: it didn't solve my problems with a magic wand but it did help. Being open with my family also meant releasing the extra burden of constantly having to carry my secret around.

The truth is that not saying anything won't actually solve anything. Think of your problems like a physical bacteria: they either need releasing or will become toxic, festering inside. Yes, recovery is scary. For me, it meant giving up something that I felt was a part of me. I didn't want to get better for a long time because I was 'the self-harming depressive in baggy band hoodies' and, without that tagline to define me, I didn't know who I was. It seemed to be a better identity than not having one at all. I was afraid of getting to know myself; that there would be nothing behind the label. And so I allowed the illness to mask the person, as I was scared of what (if anything) was beneath. To this day, I'm still genuinely surprised by the layers of compassion, tolerance, mischief and ballsiness that I found. Speaking out gives you a chance to heal yourself and, while sorrow only breeds pain, seeking help breeds success, happiness and gives you a shot to fulfil your goals.

We only get one life: the power to make it count lies in your hands.

TELLING PARENTS AND PROFESSIONALS

In order to write this chapter, we asked parents and professionals to explain what happens on the other side when someone confesses about a mental-health or personal issue.

Most parents said, 'We already knew something was wrong and were just relieved when they finally came out with it.' Some told us that, at first, they were a little scared and needed a bit of time to digest what was happening. All of them said that they'd respect their children's wishes if they said they didn't want their school to be involved.

Teachers told us that they were able to keep conversations confidential, as long they didn't involve a 'child-protection issue' (so, for example, sexual abuse). They told us they were always happy to listen but often found it hard because there are certain things they aren't allowed to say (for example, 'That happened to me once.').

We spoke to someone who works for the Samaritans (a telephone helpline) as well as The Site, which runs moderated message boards for young people (details of both at the end of this book). The upshot is that it is totally possible to talk to someone completely anonymously. When you call an organisation like Samaritans, there is nothing you can say that will cause them to call the police/doctor – they can only encourage you to seek outside help if they think you need it. You won't be forced to do anything you aren't comfortable with.

CHAPTER TWENTY

HOW DO I GET MORE CONFIDENCE?

NADZ

Sadly, there aren't any pills or potions that will magically grant you self-esteem, despite what some advertisers may try to pledge so that you buy their product. ('For just £999.99, this cream will freeze your face when you hit twenty-one years old and never change, and, if you buy the night syrup for our special offer of £499.99, you will be wealthier than Mariah Carey, Oprah and Tom Cruise put together.')

A great truth rarely shared is that you won't find self-esteem in the bottom of a wine bottle, or sewn into the label of designer clothes, nor sitting pretty at the tip of a Botox needle. Instead, that beast you're searching for can be found by accepting who you are. Acceptance means working with what you've got, rather than chasing something you're not. The art to maintaining self-esteem is to know it is a work in progress, even once you've got it. Tash, Grace and I are not immune to feeling crappy about ourselves but we are equipped with knowledge of how to pick ourselves up out the rut, should we land in one. And we've learned that, just as we work on physical health with sport, we must do workouts for the mind too.

Sounds dull but sturdy building blocks to boost confidence begin with exercise. The word 'exercise' is about as exciting as Pythagoras's Theorem. But instead of mindlessly trudging along to nowhere on the cross-trainer at Fitness First, or having to wear a headband and Lycra on a thirteen-hour hike, try something different, like bouldering, ice-skating, Parkour, a street dance class, or join a roller derby. People at school can laugh all they want but these are the sorts of activities that will make you feel like a badass and have you counting more memories in your life than calories. You don't need a science degree to know that moving more means keeping healthy, in turn helping our immune system prevent things like heart disease and diabetes. Keeping fit can also help fend off depression, which means an ability to have better body image, a more positive outlook and – drum roll, please – higher self-esteem.

Who cares if you run looking like you have two left feet (I would bet my life savings on the fact you won't)

fun. If there's one thing you take away from this book, let it be not to shy away from things because of how you could look in a tight top. Do it in pyjamas if you need to (like me when I rave at Morning Gloryville – Google it). And definitely do it for *you*, not because that gobby pundit is yelling at you from the telly box that, 'ALL FAT PEOPLE ARE LAZY AND GROSS AND SMELLY AND SHOULD BE QUARNATINED!' (One day, we will 'Self-Esteem Team' Katie Hopkins. She'll see the error of her ways as a professional troll and deliver a live, televised apology to the nation, with special reference to the obese, ginger, Muslim, poor and tattooed. We shall not rest until this happens.)

Another good stepping stone for better confidence is catching plenty of zzzzzzs. I am a far more stable individual (my boyfriend might disagree) now that I insist on a full night of snoozing, rather than surviving on an erratic two hours before work following a partying sesh – although I have been known to blame staying up all night on my job: 'But I had to go to the third club at 2.30am, twenty-five miles from home and spend half my salary on a round of drinks as I was trying to get exclusive quotes!!!' Not only does it make us less frazzled and less emotionally charged, it also helps manage stress, allows us to concentrate the next day and reduces paranoia. So if a mate doesn't text back, being sleep deprived may make you feel insecure that you've done something wrong and that they suddenly hate you, yet a well-rested mind gives you the logic to understand that they're most likely just busy.

Do stuff. Try banning yourself from social media one day a week to focus on you. Educate yourself, not with yawn textbooks but watch *vice* documentaries on YouTube. Read books so that you can write a book. You don't have to wait until you've left school to snowball your ambitions. Without going all Nike on your ass: Just. Do. It.

If you don't know what you want to do, that's fine. Spend some time figuring it out. Learn about people like Jamal Edwards. Understand that feeling good comes from inside, not from what shade of lip-gloss you wear or which brand of jeans warm your legs daily. Push yourself, chase your dreams... or else someone else will hire you so they can achieve theirs.

Write down the things you like about yourself or how you might want to better yourself. Scribble these positive affirmations on post-it notes and stick them around your mirror to give you a pep-up each morning. You don't have to construct full mini-essays – just little buzz words, like 'hope', 'believe' or 'stay strong' could be enough. OK, maybe not 'believe', unless you're a Belieber. Avoid negative people or those who try to put you down. Don't just celebrate idols, go out and defeat them.

Make a pact with your friends that you will compliment each other on non-aesthetic things, so let them know if they make you laugh or if they did something brave or supported you through a break-up. Chances are that's why you're mates with them, not because they happen to have a new pair of Louis Vuitton sunglasses.

Life is a canvas: throw all the paint and colour at it that you possibly can.

Be aware that you will have bad days and that it's totally #normal to feel blue sometimes but know how to deal with those days when they come along (family size Ben & Jerry's tub, avoid films like *Requiem For A Dream*, epic bubble bath).

Value yourself because, if you don't, someone else will decide what you are worth.

And remember – always remember – that there ain't *no* such thing as perfect.

Oh, and because we say stuff like this all the time, follow @_selfesteemteam on Twitter and Instagram. Or check out our Facebook page, The Self-Esteem Team.

BYE!

TASH

When I was thirteen, I read a book called *Thirteen Something* by Jane Goldman. You can't buy it online anymore, sadly (but I did manage to track down a copy from an independent bookshop in Norwich). It was the best thing I'd ever read – a non-patronising, funny, honest survival guide for my teenage years (sound familiar?).

One of the chapters was on things to do when you are bored. There are about fifty suggestions for activities to fill the days of a long summer holiday and one was to write a letter to your adult self.

I must have taken the advice because recently my mum found a letter I'd written, aged fifteen, to my adult self in the loft. It's hilarious (sadly not intentionally). I seemed to be mainly concerned with promising myself that one day I'd have a boyfriend and staying a size twelve. I don't remember being unduly bothered by either of these things at the time.

As I read the letter, I found myself thinking that I wished I could time travel back and say to myself, 'You will have lots of boyfriends, some of whom will be lovely and some who will be absolute bastards. The key thing is distinguishing between the two. Also, please just focus on your health and let your body do what it wants because sizes are different in different shops, so ultimately meaningless.' Then, perhaps, slap myself a bit.

In honour of that thought, Grace, Nadz and I have written letters to our teenage selves. We hope you'll find something to relate to and realise that everything will be OK, however much you might not feel like it right now.

NADZ

Hey. Hey, you. Hello? Oi, you with your shoulders stooped low. Yeah, you. That's better. Head up. Not just a body floating down the corridor, trying to blend into the walls.

Hi, Nadia.

I know it's hard to spot in the mirror right now but, where you see a loser, I see a fighter. Courage does not always roar: it's that little voice inside your head each night that says, 'I'll try again tomorrow.' Now, more than ever, you've got to turn the shit the bullies give you into fertiliser and grow from it.

Pick up a pen. Vent, vent, vent until your biro bleeds ink onto the page so you don't have to. Release those toxic emotions, spill it all into a diary, tell Mum and Dad. Articulate those feelings in writing you can't speak with your tongue. Get that pain from inside, outside.

There are a few surprises out there for you... Can you believe that those thoughts that drive you crazy will one day make you a Master of Philosophy? I know – WTf? And can you believe your inability to 'fit in' will one day help others who struggle to do the same.

So, here's a bit of tough love: life doesn't owe you a favour. Your problems won't vanish overnight. You won't be handed success for free. You must fight, like everyone else. Don't romanticise your sorrow – it will only eat at your soul. You are more than your illness.

And the number-one golden rule: ignore the haters.

You gotta lift that head of yours. Higher, baby girl. Higher.

OK, I hear you: things are hard at home, you're not exactly first on the guest list to parties and you're in the bottom sets for Maths and English (yeah, don't worry about French) but it's your stubbornness to never give up – that little thing Mum and Dad call *'chutzpah'* – that is going to get you further than any grade A. Those people at school may laugh because you're different but you should laugh because they're all the same. True friends will come soon, so keep blagging, stay true to yourself and keep seeing more bands... because one day you're going to be interviewing them for a job.

Those hands you use to cut yourself will one day craft words for you to earn a living travelling the world (and live in Venice Beach!!), that heart you've numbed with ice will one day thaw for you to fall in love, those concrete barriers you've built will come crashing down to let you inspire others. It gets better, hang on. And trust me on this (after all, I'm you).

Little one, lift your head. It's time to put down the blade now.

Love, Nadz xxxx

GRACE

Dear Grace,

It's 11pm. Ten years have flown by and guess what you're doing? Yep, writing your diary/poems. You still do that almost every night (the drunk nights make for great reading a couple of weeks later btw) but you've stopped writing your hopes and dreams at the bottom of each page. Not because you don't have any anymore - far from it. You just decided a little while ago to take the pressure off. Anyway, where you are now, those dreams include play Glastonbury Festival, have three children (twin boys and a girl), meet Mike Skinner, sing like Beyoncé, buy a house, live in London and LA, design your own clothes and more. I also know you've affixed a time frame to it. You want to have a successful music career by twenty-one because then you can buy a house and start a family by twenty-five.

So you'd probably be horrified to hear that, at twenty-five, you don't have your own home, you don't have kids (or even a boyfriend) and your international global fame is, let's just say, not quite at Beyoncé levels. But you are happy.

You have more strength than you're aware of yet. Your tenacity, your drive and your bounce-back ability will surprise everyone, including yourself at times. You'll be right not to give up.

But it's important to know not to use your own strength against yourself. You're doing OK. You're moving quick enough, you're making progress. Don't get in your own way so much. I won't tell you to be patient - you'd hate that (and, just for the record, you still don't believe it's a virtue; maybe you never will) but look up and smell the roses every now and then.

Knowing what you want in life already will prove to be both a blessing and a curse. Maybe let the universe take over for a while. Live. Do things that don't immediately seem to equal success or progress. Experience things just because.

You will do things you never dreamed of; things that actually help you to know more about who you are. Let them in, attack them with your trademark enthusiasm and revel in their lessons, then see where you end up.

Love, your twenty-five-year-old, Glastonbury Festival playing, no baby having, book-writing (who knew!?), London-living self.

TASH
Dear Tash,

First of all, thank you for loving school so much and trying so hard to do your best. I still find uses for the knowledge and skills you are learning, right now.

I want to reassure you that you are, fundamentally, a good person. Because I know that you sometimes wonder if you are. In fact, you have a huge propensity for kindness and bravery... But you aren't always right. I know you think you are. You're not. Sorry.

The world isn't black and white as you

imagine it to be. You understand a lot in theory but the practice of living is very different. Not everything you need to know can be learned from books. Opinions shouldn't be set in stone and it doesn't make you weak if you revise one of yours. Life is not divided up into heroes and villains. People do bad things but it doesn't make them bad people.

Over the next few years, you will do bad things and the hardest part of your development will be learning how to forgive yourself.

The demons you battle are also your greatest strengths. So, yes, your relentless propensity for perfectionism and slightly OCD nature, combined with a contradictory 'aw, fuck it' stance on risk-taking is going to land you in some hot water in your immediate future. But later, you will learn to turn perfectionism into drive and headstrongness into courage.

You'll still fuck up sometimes. At the time of writing, just yesterday you accused one of the major political party leaders of being 'a bit like Hitler' on live, national television. (He was being a bit like Hitler but you should have found a less offensive way of phrasing your objections.) The difference between you then and now is that today you have the humility to admit your mistakes. (Luckily for you, it's an incredibly fast-paced world and your gaffe was soon forgotten because a lady called Kim Kardashian changed her hair colour... I don't have time right now to explain why that's so important).

You don't have to mould yourself to fit your environment. You can listen to and like spending time with someone without agreeing with everything they say and do. Trust yourself a bit more. You will try out various incarnations of yourself over the decade that follows but you'll eventually end up right back where you started – a bit chubby, red-haired, either giggling uncontrollably at something daft, having a strong opinion, or a combination of the two. It's who you are.

Most of all, I want to tell you that you can decide how to live. These life rules that you imagine exist are self-imposed and fuelled by entities that want to control you. (Pay more attention during Mr Biggins' lesson on modern propaganda. He's right.)

The current sphere you inhabit is tiny and the world outside is almost infinitely diverse. You will meet people who will teach you that the ways to be happy and successful aren't as fixed and linear as you thought. But, ultimately, it's down to you.

You'll be fine.

Love,

Tash

PS: That teacher who told you you'd never make it as a professional writer because your style isn't succinct enough was talking bollocks.

FURTHER SOURCES OF HELP AND INFORMATION

To find out more about The Self-Esteem Team, go to www.selfesteemteam.org.

We can bring lessons on things like body image, self-harm, coping with difficult feelings and dealing with exam stress into your school, college or uni. We also have Associate Lecturers who do presentations on a wide variety of other topics you might want to learn about.

Young Minds – The UK's leading charity committed to improving the emotional wellbeing and mental health of children and young people – http://www.youngminds.org.uk/

The Site – Confidential online webchat forum to get advice and support on mental health.

Samaritans – Confidential helpline for any kind of worry – 08457 90 90 90

Head Meds – Information for young people on mental-health medication – www.headmeds.org.uk

Rethink Mental Illness – Challenging attitudes around mental health – www.rethink.org

B-eat – National charity supporting people affected by eating disorders – www.b-eat.co.uk

Men Get Eating Disorders Too – Support for men with eating disorders – www.mengetedstoo.co.uk

The Cybersmile Foundation – Tackling all forms of online bullying/hate campaigns – www.cybersmile.org

National Self-Harm Network – Support and advice for those affected by self-harm – www.nshn.co.uk

OCD UK – Working with children and adults affected by OCD – www.ocduk.org

Beat Bullying – International bullying-prevention charity – www.beatbullying.org

Beyond Chocolate – Advice and workshops on mindful eating – www.beyondchocolate.co.uk

Body Gossip – A charity promoting body confidence – www.bodygossip.org

Make Love Not Porn – Realistic sex information and videos for young people – www.makelovenotporn.com

Scouting for Jobs – Websites to help former Scouts and Guides find employment – www.scouting4Jobs.com and www.guidingU2Jobs.com

All Walks Beyond the Catwalk – A campaign to bring more diversity into fashion advertising – www.allwalks.org

Caroline Hirons – Skin expert – www.carolinehirons.com